METHODOLOGICAL ISSUES

IN RELIGIOUS STUDIES

METHODOLOGICAL ISSUES

IN RELIGIOUS STUDIES

Edited by

Robert D. Baird

With Contributions from

Wilfred Cantwell Smith
Jacob Neusner
Hans H. Penner

NEW HORIZONS PRESS

BL
41
.M43

Printed in the U.S.A.
NEW HORIZONS PRESS
P.O. Box 1758, Chico, CA. 95926

Acknowledgment. Chapter II appears herein as presented at the symposium with
the discussion that followed. A modified version appears in *History of Religions*
(14:3, pp. 191-206) by Jacob Neusner, "The Study of Religion as the Study of
Tradition: Judaism." Used with permission of The University of Chicago Press,
copyright © 1974.

LIBRARY OF CONGRESS CATALOGING IN PUBLICATION DATA

Main entry under title:

Methodological issues in religious studies.

   Proceedings of a symposium held Apr. 15-17,
1974, at the School of Religion of the University
of Iowa.
   Includes bibliographical references.
   1. Religion—Historiography—Congresses.
2. Religions—Historiography—Congresses.
I. Baird, Robert D., 1933-   II. Smith, Wilfred
Cantwell, 1916-
BL41.M43   200'.7'2   75-44170
ISBN 0-914914-08 1
ISBN 0-914914-073 pbk.

PREFACE

On April 15-17, 1974, the School of Religion of The University of Iowa hosted a symposium on "Methodology and World Religions." Methodological considerations have long interested historians of religions, and the state of the literature seemed to indicate that no single approach to religious phenomena was dominating research of the religions of mankind. It was therefore our intention to invite three leading historians of religions who might be expected to approach religious data, and methodological issues relating to approach itself, somewhat differently. That this expectation was fulfilled is seen in the fact that one of the participants even questioned the appropriateness of the emphasis given to methodology in modern scholarship.

Professor Wilfred Cantwell Smith's approach to the study of "religion" as the study of persons has become familiar to most scholars in the field through his seminal book *The Meaning and End of Religion*. In that volume he rejected, as the legitimate goal in "religious" studies, the study of "religions" such as "Hinduism," "Buddhism," etc. Professor Jacob Neusner's approach has also become well known through his numerous books and articles. Not only is it historical, but it is directed toward the study of Judaism, one of the "religions" which Smith had rejected as the goal of religious study. Through his articles, Professor Hans Penner has shown himself to be an astute analyst of methodological problems from a more theoretical perspective. The discussion which ensued from the presentations indicates that we indeed assembled three eminent and at the same time different types of historians of religions.

Although, for the most part, the participants spoke from carefully prepared manuscripts, the point of the symposium was to offer a forum for the discussion of methodological issues. That the papers do not claim to present the final thought of the participants seemed no obstacle to the worthwhile discussion which followed the presentations, and it was the discussion provoked by the presentations that made them valuable to those who attended the symposium.

The proceedings of this symposium are offered to the scholarly public as an indication of the directions in which three historians of religions are moving in terms of methodological considerations. Each participant had ample opportunity to read the papers of the other participants prior to their presentation, and were in attendance at all lectures and seminars. The intention of such an arrangement was to enable the participants to confront the ideas of each other. It is for this reason that substantial portions of the discussions are included in this volume. On occasions the question asked of the participant may be considered less valuable than the answer given, in that the question provided the occasion for the fuller clarification of the position being stated. On other occasions the answers given to questions may be deemed by some to be inadequate or to have missed the point of the question. They are included, nevertheless, in cases where the question seemed to be quite to the point. If pointed questions were not answered adequately, then one of the merits of the symposium would become apparent, i.e., the possibility of determining where a given theory or approach required further elucidation.

In addition to the presence of faculty and students from the School of Religion of The University of Iowa, there were registrants from various parts of the United States and Canada. Their searching questions extended the discussion beyond the three participants. The papers which follow, then, along with the discussions which they provoked, open to the reader some central issues which are under debate in the scholarly study of religion in North America today. They also make available the thought processes of three eminent historians of of religions in a way which published manuscripts seldom do.

The papers appear as they were originally presented. The single exception is Professor Smith's seminar presentation: "The Meaning of Scripture: A Non-Reductionist Historian's View." That paper was given from notes, and considered by Professor Smith as too fragmentary for for publication. The panel discussion, "Is the Comparative Study of Religion Possible?" and the discussions which followed the formal presentations were transcribed from tapes and edited. Although the discussions are not included in their entirety, in no case was any thought intentionally changed or modified. The participants have had the opportunity to make minor changes of a stylistic nature. The final essay, "Postscript: Methodology, Theory and Explanation in the Study of Religion" was not presented at the symposium, but represents some thoughts of the editor on the proceedings. This essay is not to be considered the final word in the discussion, but an attempt at clarifification and a basis for still further discussion.

If the history of the scholarly study of religion gives any indication of its future course, it is unlikely that this symposium or any subsequent one will finalize methodological issues for all time. Just as the content of religious study changes from one generation of scholars to another, so do the approaches which they utilize in dealing with that content. But what these papers and discussions do is to raise some interesting issues which are being considered by the present generation of scholars.

The editor wishes to thank the Director of the School of Religion, Professor James C. Spalding, for his support for this project, and the faculty of the School for their interest in such themes. Special recognition must also be accorded to Ms. Mary Lou Doyle, Editorial Assistant in the School of Religion, for her handling of many of the details surrounding this symposium, and for her continued assistance in preparing the manuscript for publication.

Robert D. Baird, Editor

TABLE OF CONTENTS

I

METHODOLOGY AND THE STUDY OF RELIGION: SOME MISGIVINGS

Wilfred Cantwell Smith

Among the Chinese, one of my best friends is a thoroughly delightful character whom many of you doubtless know too—and probably admire, perhaps almost as much as do I. I know him only through writing, but he puts so much of his personality into his written words that this is a relatively minor limitation. He is a marvellously warm-hearted chap, and on hearing that I had been invited to Iowa to participate in this symposium he generously offered to write my opening speech for me, or rather to let me use something that he had written on the same subject a fair while ago, but he felt, and I agree, that it is still pertinent. I refer to Chuang Tzu, the 3rd-century-B.C. Taoist poet-philosopher; and specifically to his winsome piece about the legendarily beautiful lady Hsi Shih. The story that he tells runs as follows, in Arthur Waley's translation:

> Once when Hsi Shih, the most beautiful of women, was frowning and beating her breast, an ugly woman saw her and thought, "Now I have found out how to become beautiful!" So she went home to her village and did nothing but frown and beat her breast. When the rich men of the village saw her, they bolted themselves into their houses and dared not come out; when the poor people of the village saw her they took wife and child by the hand and ran at top speed. This woman had seen that someone frowning was beautiful and thought that she had only to frown in order to become beautiful.

I love this vignette, and its enabling us to see vividly for ourselves the absurdity of the false position that he ridicules, and his deftly

1

emphasizing it by depicting those hapless villagers scrambling to flee from the sorry sight. This is sheer genius; and I thought for a time of simply stopping there, claiming that Chuang Tzu had said long ago all that need or can be said on our topic. Surely his anecdote presents with charm, but also with force, the ludicrousness of supposing that methodology is decisive or even significant; that if someone does something well, all that the rest of us need do is to follow that person's method and all will be fine. In human affairs, he eloquently reminds us, method is at best incidental, at all times potentially distracting, and if one is not careful can degenerate into fatuity.

If I go on, it is not that I can add anything to the wit or to the penetration of the Chinese master; but rather in order that I may learn something. Chuang Tzu puts the above story in the mouth of the music-master Chin speaking to Yen Hui, a disciple of K'ung Fu Tzu, as part of his playful but sustained needling of the Confucians. I have myself needled the formalists more than once, and laughed at them, which is healthy since I myself am at heart a formalist; but in my deeper heart I know that a wise man is *both* a Confucian and a Taoist, and I have come today not to scoff but to learn. If Professor Baird will allow me to disclose this, I may confess that when he first did me the honour to invite me to this gathering I declined, as simply one more expression of my long-standing reservations, and indeed obtuseness, on the methodology question. I was inclined to plead incompetence, convinced that this is not my field, and presumably therefore not my conference. Within 24 hours, however, I was on the phone to him again, asking if he would allow me after all to come. For I realized that here might well be my golden opportunity to educate myself in this realm.

For many years I have been restless—of late, increasingly so—on this methodology matter, feeling myself at a very great distance from my fellows on the modern university scene. And I have realized that it is high time that I endeavour to clarify to myself, at least, and perhaps even to others, what the issues are between me and the rest of academia. It seemed wise to attempt to articulate my misgivings, not to say my distress, my alienation, in the hopes that I could begin finally to make some progress towards clearing up the confusions. For it has become quite evident that I am unusually obtuse on this point. Manifestly something is wrong when virtually all my friends, and many persons obviously much more intelligent than I, are stalwart methodologists, whereas I feel that methodology is the massive red herring of modern scholarship, the most significant obstacle to intellectual progress, and the chief distraction from rational understanding of the world.

These are very strong words. I state the point starkly so to make clear that the gulf is wide, and appears also to be deep. Obviously, I have not understood what is meant by "methodology," or I should not feel this way about it. Obviously, I have not made myself understood, when I think I see the primary values of humane scholarship threatened by it, else my friends would have salvaged me from my errors ere now (or I them from theirs).

If there be any perspicacity in my position, there has certainly been no perspicuity.

I have come to Iowa in the hopes of learning what is so wrong with my understanding of scholarship in the humanities, or my formulation of it, or my perception of my colleagues' formulations. In this presentation, I am making a serious effort to formulate my reservations. I hope that I can make these sufficiently clear as to be intelligible; and I would plead with you to help me to see where I am wrong, insofar as I am. Let me at the outset make what may seem a concession. When I affirm that the emphasis on method in modern university thinking disturbs or alienates me, I have to admit to myself that I too in some sense prize method, and stress it, and give loyalty to it; and I expect my students to do so. Now that I am teaching undergraduates, I find myself devoting much time and effort to hammering away in an attempt to inculcate method, especially in written work submitted—and rigorously. Yet there is a difference here. For when I think and feel this way, I have in mind the academic method generically. It pertains to intellectual inquiry all 'round, and underlies the university as such. First and foremost, it is rational; and there are many other attributes that one might list: it is critical, analytical, systematic, deliberate, comparative, public, cumulative. It is inductive, and in some sense empirical. One could prolong the list. There are more specific matters also, such as acknowledging indebtedness rather than plagiarizing, and giving exact rather than vague references when citing authorities, and so on. Involved are a scrupulous attention to detail; fastidious precision in the reporting of it; relentless honesty.

Nevertheless, except for the fact that mathematics would seem to be an exception to the inductive-empirical matter, this academic method is, as I have said, generic for *all* university studies; it is not particular, differing from discipline to discipline.

In other words, in my vision of academic procedure and rational inquiry there is no specific method for one subject differentiating it from another. Academic method is what all scholars have in common, not what differentiates them. (We shall be returning to this.)

A second point, also weighty, is that this general academic method is preamble, is subordinate. A good academic learns it, assimilates it, forgets it—in the sense that it is taken so much for granted that he moves on from there to the substance of his work. Ideally, he absorbs it to the point where he is unconscious of it, not self-conscious about it.

My divergence, and my restlessness, then, on this issue, are much deeper than most of my friends can understand. For the divergence, I think of three possible explanations: a geographic, a chronological, and what some might call a "disciplinary." For the first: I come out of a university tradition historically derived from Britain, whereas the recent academic patterns of this country intellectually derive from Germany. This might explain how it is that, after happy years in Canada, Britain, and India, I was never able to feel quite intellectually at home in this country. Another way of seeing the issue would be as a polarity between the old and the new. This could make my understanding of scholarship, which I might be predisposed to call a traditional or even a classical view, rather that of an old fogey: the outlook of a person who has simply not caught up with modern intellectual developments. Still a third interpretation would analyse the difference between my position and the prevalent one as fundamentally a divergence between the humane and the natural sciences. According to this view, concepts and orientations derived from, and presumably appropriate to, the natural sciences would have been taken over into the study of human affairs; by the social sciences deliberately and proudly—they explicitly boast that they are imitating the natural sciences in their methods and outlooks—and even by many humanists, under the great weight of the prestige of the natural, and nowadays perhaps also the social, sciences.

I should guess that all three of these interpretations probably hold some water; that all are relevant. None of them contributes anything however, to determining what is right and what is wrong; what legitimate, and what damaging. The stress on methodology and "discipline" may have become strong because of German, or of contemporary, or of natural science influences; and yet any or all of these might be reasons why it was to be deplored, as well as why it was to be applauded. Whatever the reasons, my vision of authentic humane scholarship and the pursuit of a genuinely rational interpretation of the world seems to lean towards a substantially different conceptualization from the currently dominant one; and I am looking for rational, rather than circumstantial, arguments as to why I should adopt a different one, one that seems to me to bode ill for our enterprise.

Let me look just a little more closely at those three possible grounds for divergence. On the first, I have little to say, since I do not know enough about the history of universities over the past century and am far from confident about interpreting what little I know. I have no reason to affirm that the British universities in the early part of this century were better than the German, nor vice versa. It might be possible to argue that the Germans were probably better on the scientific side; and it was primarily in this respect that the modern American university has been continuous with the German, especially at the turn of the century. So far as the humanities are concerned: British scholarship had its distinctive qualities; and I suppose that one could say that the Germans' was characterized on the one hand by their philosophic idealism, and on the other by a greater stress on technical depth. In the U.S. development, the idealism ambiance was dropped, a pragmatist outlook to some degree substituted. Formally, the British universities put their best eggs into the undergraduate honours school basket, the American theirs into the new Ph.D. program, which may have contributed something to a greater hatching of sophisticated techniques not only in the natural sciences but in the humanities, and an emphasis on them, and on technique as such. I should be grateful if any of you can enlighten me on these matters. Am I right in thinking that concepts like "discipline" and "methodology," which were virtually unheard words, I believe, in Oxford, Cambridge, Edinburgh, Toronto, the Panjab, and the like between the two World Wars, came to prevail in the United States from the German heritage? I myself am not even well enough informed in these matters to know whether this question is worth pursuing. There is a further question: even if the German source be so, whether after the trans-Atlantic transplant this orientation to scholarship has been carried further, and become more technocratic, operationalistic, under the influence of the enormously successful and highly operationalist technological capitalism of this country. The social system here in this country, constituting the environment for academic as for other developments, with its impressive corporate structures and large-scale industrial and governmental planning, has been on the whole more efficient than humane, perhaps; more attuned to methodological prowess and procedural organization, whether in dealing with things or with persons, than to a concern for appreciating the humanity of the men and women whom it treats.

   On the chronological matter, I speak with more confidence. Whatever the cultural or sociological provenance, the temporal sequence is clear. There would seem no question but that there has been, over the last several decades, a powerful shift in academic studies from *subject-matter* to *discipline*. Let no one underestimate the deep significance of that development. I invite you to join me in deploring it; or at the very least, to join me in ferreting out and considering some of its implications.

The faculty members of a university used to divide up their work among themselves according to differing objects of investigation; more recently, by differing methods of investigation. It was assumed in the former case that each scholar would find methods that were appropriate, fruitful, to his field; in the latter case, that each will find things to examine that are presumably appropriate to his methods. Classically, one department was discriminated from another by what it studied; nowadays, by how it studies.

As I understand it, a Ph.D. in, for instance, anthropology, is in a certain sense a certification that the recipient has learned the methods of anthropology, has demonstrated that he knows how to apply them, and is launched on the world with this equipment. What makes him an anthropologist is his grasp of those methods and his reliability in applying them. Once he has them, he may apply them wherever he finds them applicable. In the old days, when anthropology was a subject, it tended to study "primitive" societies on remote islands. Now that it is a discipline, its methods may be applied to an investigating of the local stamp club, a women's political movement, the Trobriand Islanders, or whatever.

Now not all departments of an Arts faculty have become "disciplines" in this sense. English literature, for example, may or might develop certain procedures peculiar to it; nonetheless it is defined by the content of its subject matter, and cannot be defined by its procedures. The Classics, again, are distinguished from any other part of the Arts faculty by the boundaries of what they study; boundaries in time and space, and to some extent in language. The method by which they study what they study is totally undefined; they may bring to bear upon their data any methods, which they themselves or anybody else may have dreamed up, that prove rewarding. It follows not only that their activity is not characterized by any specific method, but also that the criterion of whether a given method is appropriate or not is the pragmatic one of whether it helps to illuminate within their field that in which at a given moment they are interested. The method used not only cannot define their work, but neither can it justify it. A scholar in the Classics must at every point justify whatever method it be that he brings to bear, not only by its theoretical but also its practical legitimacy, in actually advancing his and his readers' knowledge and understanding of the subject matter. If upon data from the classical world he brings to bear the methods of Freudian psychoanalysis, Marxian economics, Thomist metaphysics, chemical carbon-dating, McLuhan literary criticism, or anything else, or thinks up new methods *ad hoc*, this is fine insofar as, and only insofar as, it advances the world's knowledge of and insight into that classical world. This means, *inter alia*, that the use of method is always under judgment by something outside itself. Hence the scholar becomes (incidentally) critical of method; but not idolatrous of it.

I once met a young American social scientist in India who was studying the role there of Muslims in political parties. I pointed out to him that in one of his studies, of an election, as reported in an interesting article that he had given me to read, he had omitted consideration of something that, I suggested, though subtle, was of quite central importance for an understanding of Muslim behaviour, including this instance. He responded, in a quite casual and unruffled manner, that his methods were unable to handle matters of that kind, and therefore he had left them out. He said this without embarrassment, without weeping, without resigning his academic appointment.

What has happened to our universities, when presumably reputable members of them will admit without blushing that their work distorts—deliberately, knowingly—what it purports to describe?

Now there are two possible answers to this sort of criticism, I suppose. One is that since sociology explicitly and admittedly is limited in its apprehensions, a full understanding of, let us say, Muslim political behaviour in India would be given by inter-disciplinary study. I shall return to this point in a moment. The other answer (not unrelated) that an apologist might give for the situation that I have just criticized might be that the sociologist in describing the political behaviour of Muslims in India is not, strictly, aspiring to describe, to represent, to understand that particular behaviour, but is aspiring rather to construct eventually theories of political behaviour generally; so that the role of this particular study, concerning this particular group of persons in India at this particular election, was aimed at contributing to an eventual universal theory of political behaviour of all men everywhere. One must in the meantime, he would concede, take note of peculiar people like Muslims, and special countries like India, in order to refine that theory, in order that the universal, abstract truth to which one aspires be not gross, over-simplified, premature. And even that final abstract truth might remain in principle unattainable; yet the business of sociology is supposed to be to approximate ever closer and closer to it, since sociology is a "science." (By the way, maybe the man was a political scientist rather than a sociologist; I do not exactly remember, and it makes no difference.)

It seems to me that the aspiration here is not a knowledge of the real world, but an abstract formula. I suppose that I was offended partly because the chap emerged as not really interested in either the Muslims or in India. His interest was in sociological theory.

The interest in abstract theory rather than in concrete actuality, in universal generalization rather than particular fact, reminds some people of science. Let me turn, then, to the third matter in the analysis of the methodological enthusiasm: the influence of the natural sciences. Those who champion the new orientation often argue that it is more scientific.

It is not at all clear to me that this is true. I speak without confidence in this realm, and am cautious in making assertions but also in accepting them. It is my impression that it is the social sciences, or more limitedly even the behavioural sciences, rather than the natural sciences that are the source of this particular malady. Some social scientists (not all, by any means) have elaborated a thesis as to how to acquire knowledge about human affairs, and have labelled it scientific, and have urged it against us humanists and against more classical social scientists. It is also my impression, which I am prepared to discuss quite spiritedly, that the position on the study of man that I champion is in fact more scientific than the one that I reject: both in the sense of being a closer parallel to the natural sciences' studies, and in the sense of being more likely to be acknowledged as such by natural scientists. If students of religion proceed on a rigorously humanist base, oriented primarily to the reality that they study, and secondly to interpreting what is observed in theories always and in principle open to revision in the light of the facts, and with method drastically subordinate to the matters under investigation and to the questions being asked, I should be inclined to predict that in that case our university colleagues in the natural sciences would recognize our work as academically not merely legitimate but indeed as substantially parallel to theirs; that an accusation of being unscientific would come not from them but from behavioural scientists; and even, that the natural scientists would acknowledge our, humanists', work as in fact more closely comparable to theirs than is the work of the methodological enthusiasts among the self-styled social or behavioural sciences.

This prediction is open to empirical testing, and I am of course prepared to find that I may be wrong. However such an opinion poll might turn out, I would still myself contend that, the natural sciences having proven themselves prodigiously successful in doing what they set out to do, studying the natural world, a true recognition on our part as humanists of their marvellously effective work, and a true emulation of it, would lie in our developing ways and means, outlooks and ideas, as appropriate to the study of man as theirs have been to the study of physical objects.

Yet in any case I insist that it does not really matter: the test of our validity in not whether we are scientific, nor whether we can establish a claim to be so; but whether we are successful in knowing and in understanding and in making intelligible man's religious life. Our duty, as members of the university, is not to be scientific, but to be rational—in ways appropriate to our subject matter—and effective.

This subject matter, which is human, is so profoundly different from the subject matter of the natural sciences, the physical world, and especially in the religious dimension of our immensely complicated, subtle human life, that it would be a dereliction of our duty if, rather than working out our own principles of study, we were to settle for simply importing notions from a radically other field. However "scientific" the methodological obsession may be, or may appear to be, if it gets in the way of our understanding what we are supposed to be studying, as I fear that it may, then it is out of place in our work.

To subordinate one's understanding of man to one's understanding of science is inhumane, inept, irrational, unscientific.

It is unscientific in a double sense. For apart from the question of the ultimate inherent difference between man and merely physical objects, there is the preliminary fact that there is more to science itself than technology. No wonder, then, that there is much more to the humanities than technique.

Humane knowing—the knowledge of man by man—is an exercise in the meeting between persons, be it across the centuries or across the world. It is, therefore, not technical, not subordinate to methodological rules. In personal relations, whether face-to-face or mediated by man's symbolic forms of expression, the use of technical procedures, unless rigorously subordinated to primarily personalist considerations, is not merely inappropriate but potentially disruptive. Man cannot know man except in mutuality: in respect, trust, and equality, if not ultimately love.

Thus it is not only that the methodology concern seems more interested in ideas than in the real world. It is also that when applied to the real world it is in danger of subordinating it to men's ideas, and even purposes. The prominence in recent Western thought given to the concept of method in epistemology goes back perhaps to Descartes, who in his fundamentally non-scientific, non-humble search for indubitable, absolute knowledge took as his model mathematics, thus focusing not on the objective world and empirical reality and on observation but on logical constructs, on ideas, and pure theory. Yet in its modern version, the outlook is not contemplative but utilitarian. It smacks of Aristotle's practical intellect, rather than theoretical. Bacon, inaugurating the scientific age, said that knowledge is power; Socrates, inaugurating the humanistic age, said that knowledge is virtue. The notion of method, the interest in methodology, smack to me of Bacon here, rather than of Socrates. Certainly they smack of Buber's I-It rather than his I-Thou. It is my impression, as I have suggested, that the best scientists are themselves not technicians, but profoundly human; reverent in the fact of an awesomely given universe. They are primarily oriented to reality, not to ideas. And their knowledge is a virtue.

However that may be, we in the humane sectors betray our task if we adopt an orientation to knowledge as technique, lending itself to manipulation and control, even to prediction (which infringes human dignity and freedom). The generating of that kind of scientific knowledge that is deliberately conceived as available to be applied, is not our task. The goal of the humanities is to know and to understand; may one not say that knowledge for understanding differs from knowledge for use?

Let me report another incident from my experience in Asia, this time from Lebanon, and with an anthropologist whom I met. This gentleman, a Westerner, admitted to me quite bluntly that he was in fact not at all interested in his Lebanese villagers as persons, nor indeed in the Middle East as an area. He had come out for a year's research from this country, he said, in order to test in that village in Lebanon certain general theories that the discipline of anthropology back home had formulated; he hoped to use his findings to confirm, to rebut, or more probably to refine those theories, and at the end of his year he would return to his academic appointment in this country, publish his results, and hope because of them to get a promotion, or at least a raise in salary. His ambition was by means of his publications to advance his own academic career; simultaneously to advance the so-called "science" of anthropology. (The concept of "academic career," by the way, is a recent development, and a very sad one.) In other words, this intellectual was using persons for his own private purposes, or for the purposes of advancing Western science. This, I feel deeply in either case, is immoral—not to say, sinful.

Now that that man was wicked is perhaps only incidentally interesting; there are many wicked persons on earth, and you might feel that it would distract us if we took time off to lament that fact. Germane to our discussion, however, are two points. One is that the sinfulness was built into his methodology; built in, one might say, to the fact that he made method dominant in his study of persons. We all fall short of ideals; but let us not have ideals that inherently exploit: conceptual frameworks that perceive the relations between persons (in this case knower and known) as technical, mechanical. That there is a method for dealing with persons goes along with the public relations ethos, with the manipulative, with the depersonalization of modern society; but surely it is to be deplored on the academic scene. If you feel that it is going simply too far to assert that the proper relation among persons is love, may we not at least agree that it includes respect, interest, openness, humility? A conception of the academic task, insofar as it involves a study of human beings that stresses method over subject matter is immoral.

Do some of you find that argument irrelevant? Some of my alarm stems from the drift of modern academic study away from moral considerations, as in the increasing use of deliberate deception in psychological and other experiments with human beings: intellectual dishonesty is not scientifically wrong, I suppose that Millman, or Darley and Batson, would say. Even if you do find the moral question irrelevant, however, there is an intellectual facet to the same consideration. The procedure-oriented approach to persons is not merely morally wrong, it is wrong intellectually. For it so happens that human beings are that kind of creature that cannot in fact be understood unless recognized as human, as personal, and treated humanely. To perceive persons as entities, contributing to more rarified theories, is inherently to misunderstand those persons—and therefore, to produce bad theories.

No art historian can be true who does not love his subject. No student of a great scholar of French literature will be as competent as is his teacher, if he has learned all the techniques but none of the appreciation, the sheer affection for the material. Polanyi feels that personal involvement is central even to the natural sciences; certainly in the study of religion, I would distrust any scholar of the Hindus who did not love India, or any interpreter of Islamics who had no Muslim friends.

It so happens that we live in the sort of universe where knowing what concerns man involves more than knowing how to proceed.

Let us turn, then, to that "interdisciplinary" question, proffered as a possible solution to the fact that every methodology inevitably omits something. It is possible that all methodologies put together would still omit something distinctly human. And indeed it is the suspicion that the characteristically religious dimension of human life has in fact proven elusive in even multi-disciplinary projects, that has led some to hope that the study of religion would provide a new methodology out of whose mechanical net this elusive human quality could somehow at last be guaranteed not to escape. The subtle, however, the elusive, the distinctly human, is what formalized method is calculated not to apprehend. The characteristically human is not accessible to technical devices; and most of all, the religious does not lend itself to formalized impersonalism. "We cannot engineer our way into the sacred," as I have heard a colleague put it.

Since I reject the concept "discipline," then, I am hardly mollified by the "interdisciplinary" gambit. The concept "interdisciplinary" I regard as at best a ladder that may help some to climb out of a hole into which the true humanist has never fallen, and I think it important not to fall. It does at least recognize that something is awry with the notion, and the practice, of "discipline." It fails to recognize, however, what that something awry is.

This fact is somewhat demonstrated in that social scientists, each recognizing that his own methodology needs supplementing in order to arrive at a valid understanding of any concrete thing (as distinct from some abstract theory), nonetheless is inclined to add to his own, in his multi-disciplinary projects, only other social-science disciplines, leaving out humanities studies of the same topic. Or, if they be included, he wishes their results in a form that he can "use"; that is, in order for them to be serviceable he insists that they be conformed to his over-all categories. For his purposes, humane knowledge must be abstracted, depersonalized, rendered technical and detachable. The contribution must conform to the notion that knowledge is technical.

It is not that I reject multi-lateral approaches; or that the classical humanist was in any sense tempted to do so. On the contrary: in the classical view of studying "subject," the problem was solved before it arose. The traditional British academic concept of an undergraduate "Honours" course, for example, has recently been criticized as overly specialized. (The University of Toronto, for instance, has recently abandoned this pattern, and on these grounds.) In fact, however, it was specialized in an older sense of concentrating on something specific and objective, but not in the modern sense of concentrating on only one aspect or dimension of, as it were, everything. Thus the student in Honours History might "specialize," to use that term, in, let us say, English history generally and specifically in the 17th century or the city of London in the decade of the 1640's; but he was expected, and encouraged, to look at whatever it was that he was thus concentratedly looking at with as much and as diverse assistance as he could muster from the psychological, the numismatic, the art-historical, or whatever.

Let us return to my example of the sociologist in India, for whom knowledge was not a knowledge of India, concretely, not of Muslims, personally, but a knowledge ideally of sociology, of theory. I would contend that no matter how many bits of knowledge of this type one might add together, one would still not arrive at a knowledge of that particular Muslim situation in India—nor indeed, of any other particular situation. I used never to understand how the mediaeval philosophers could consider the possibility that God could know anything, without knowing particulars. I am equally perplexed by a notion of sciences of man that might consist of spectacularly brilliant, and even in some sense true, theories, but that did not take the form of a direct knowledge (*connaissance* rather than *savoir*) of human history, in its actuality, diversity, and solidity.

We are becoming involved here in a philosophic issue with which I have been wrestling some of late: the problem of epistemology and of truth, and the nature of knowledge. Especially at issue is whether the object of man's knowledge is a proposition, or a state of affairs. There is perhaps a modern tendency to favour the former; and if knowledge is of propositions, there is a further question as to whether we approach closer to or recede further from true knowledge as the proposition becomes more generalized, more abstract.

Also at issue is the question of analysis and synthesis. The natural sciences found for a time that their knowledge advanced by their focusing on more and more distinct areas of inquiry. The smallest unit of human affairs, the individual person, the atom of the humane sciences, however, is more complicated than anything else in the universe. More-over, not only are we complicated; we integrate. However fine our analysis, we cannot understand man unless we understand synthesis.

The point here is that in humane study it is the individual student who is expected to do the integrating. A well-educated man, in the classical model, was one who understood the complexity, and multi-valence, of every human affair; while the good scholar was he who could illuminate that affair, in its complexity and multi-valence. As he went on in depth, he learned more and more not about a particular method, but about a particular thing.

Thus, let us take an example from our own field, a study of the *Hajj*, the Pilgrimage to Makkah. A good historian of religion will learn all that he can learn from any insights that are or can be made to be pertinent: sociological, philological, historical, psychological, typological (sometimes called "phenomenological"), introspective, and to add something of my own, asking Muslims—and many more. Indeed, he will use these approaches, and not merely profit from others' use of them. Yet what he has specialized upon is something in the real world: namely, the *Hajj*. I have been called a methodological pluralist. Rather, I take methods so lightly that I hardly deserve to have it so dignified. When Bleeker speaks of a "right" methodology for "the science of Religion," I quake.

We have come, then, to the specific matter of the study of religion. So far I have been talking rather about methodology and the humanities at large, where I claim that the methodological emphasis threatens to disrupt knowledge, to distort it, and to obstruct understanding. Certainly my feeling that an academic department is best characterized in terms of what it studies, not how, comes saliently into play in our own particular academic enterprise.

In many universities, the question as to whether there should be a religion department in the Liberal Arts faculty was interpreted as asking, essentially, does the study of religion have its own methodology. Fortunately it does not; and I can think of nothing more calculated to damage the academic study of religion than its acquiring one, whether out of pressure to appear respectable among colleagues, or whether out of a genuine supposition that this is a good way to study human affairs. Given the uniquely subtle, elusive, volatile quality of the religious, it is surely probable that the one thing that we are most desirous of attempting to understand in our study would be precisely what would be omitted by any formalized, pre-conceived procedure or, more subtly, by our relying on any procedure; supposing, as it were, that it could do our work for us.

On this particular point I chuckled to myself over the fact that one of the most major, and most definitely *religious*, attainments of my own scholarly study in Islamics, the understanding of the meaning of the word *islam* and its relation to the concept "religion," I arrived at in part by the somewhat mechanical, although in the end revealing, procedure of going through a list of 25,000 book-titles in Arabic, arranged in alphabetical order, and listing in chronological order the 84 titles that I culled from among them in which the Arabic word *islam* occurs. It amuses me to think how excessively stupid it would be if I were to teach my students, or if anybody else were to imagine, that the way to arrive at insight in religious matters is to count book-titles! Page Chuang Tzu and that ugly woman . . . . Any scholar worth his salt would surely be too proud to follow any one else's method, too humble to suppose that others would wish to follow his, to say nothing of too engrossed in his subject matter to be distracted by generic theorizing about abstractions. Method should be developed out of the particular problem that one is considering, not vice versa, and it should be ephemeral, subordinate, and fundamentally dispensable. If the result at which I arrived were not able to be confirmed by totally different procedures, and indeed were it not able to have been arrived at in the first place through some drastically other method equally well, then I should regard its conclusions as unreliable.

In fact, in the religious field, so prone are outsiders to misinterpret that I myself always feel decidedly tentative about any conclusion until I have double- and triple-checked. (And may we not accent the point that it is not the method that I check, but the results?)

Indeed, might we not set up as a principle that the validity of the result reached by any particular method, a question much exercising the methodological enthusiasts, is tested best not merely by evaluating that method, rationally and for aptness, but by ascertaining whether those results are convincing judged by other criteria, including whether they are confirmed by a quite other method?

This is doubly so, in that particular results are in fact never reached simply as a result of using a given method. Much more is involved than that. The Dutch scholar van der Leeuw wrote a quite good book called originally *Phenomenology of Religion*. (That phrase became a sub-title in the English-language version, which, since it was published in England, was called primarily *Religion in Essence and Manifestation*.) Because he had accomplished something quite significant in this particular study, a number of people rushed about to seize upon his method, and felt that if they copied it, they too would write good books. So far has this now gone that Phenomenology of Religion itself has become a subject of study, we shall return to this. Meanwhile, one may simply note that those who copied this Dutchman's method seemed not to ask themselves about his person, his sensitivity, his intelligence, his insightfulness, his sympathy, and so on. Indeed, I am left wondering whether the emphasis on method is not designed to relieve us of as much of the personal as possible, in the hopes of by-passing the really difficult challenges. Into the writing of a book of that kind goes a whole series of factors, of which it is surely obvious that method is only one, and of which it is not at all obvious that it is anywhere near the top in order of importance.

It would seem to me relatively easy to argue, and indeed to demonstrate, that the attitude, the philosophy, and the general orientation of an author are of major consequence for any scholarly study; are at least equally important, and usually more important, than the method employed. I speak a little tentatively here, because it seems to me that some of my friends talk about methodology when they mean not something pertaining to method but what I would call, rather, conceptual framework, ideology, presuppositions, or the like. The preconceptions with which any scholar approaches any given problem or task undoubtedly colour the conclusions to which he comes. I am inclined, accordingly, to give a great deal of attention, in the critical appraisal of academic work, to this matter of conceptual starting-point. In one's own work, and in the educating of students who come into our field, one may well stress the matter of being self-conscious about one's preconceptions and ideological stance. Often, in fact, a given method is almost predictably derived from the preconceptions of the person using it. (In passing, I may elaborate this to remark that, in illustration, the behavioural sciences' stress on methodology is itself a product of the, to my mind, fundamentally false preconceptual framework of the behavioural sciences.)

I said just now that when a significant book appears in our field, there is a tendency to pounce upon its method and to focus upon that, for imitation by all concerned. The fad even goes to the point of setting it up for separate study itself. Thus "the Phenomenology of Religion" has become something that is studied as such, even though there be nothing in the objective world to which that rubric is the corresponding intellectualization. To study phenomenology of religion is not to study the real world. Or, if that be going too far, let me put it this way: that to study phenomenology of religion is to turn from an interest in the centuries-long history of religion in Asia and to concern oneself with the recent history of thought in Europe instead. Phenomenology is a minor movement in Western thought, interesting to people who happen to be interested in that sort of thing; but it should be dealt with as a particular subject matter, ancillary to the study of religion itself.

Last September the Department of Religion at Columbia University wrote to me, and I presume to others, saying that they were "looking for a person with a clear grasp of methodological issues in the study of religion, with interest in specific contemporary methods such as phenomenology and structuralism, who also has an area of depth in specific forms of religious phenomena." One may note here the primary interest in method, with substantive knowledge as an additive extra, rather than vice versa. They did not wish someone who knew a particular religious tradition, or any other concrete empirical matters primarily, and "who also has" a competence in questions of method; but the other way 'round. Some universities, similarly, make a course on phenomenology of religion an introductory freshman offering (though van der Leeuw himself admitted to his course on that subject only doctoral candidates in their final year of study).

I am not unaware that there are counterparts to this in other sectors of the modern university; yet neither am I sure but that the drift of these, too, is perhaps to be deplored, or at least sharply questioned. At the university where I now am, in Canada, Sociology 100, the only freshman course in that field available in next year's catalogue, is an introduction not to human society, but to sociology as a discipline, with theory primary and the matter being studied secondary. If you think I misrepresent, listen to the course description:

> Sociology 100 is designed to provide both a general intro-
> duction to the discipline of sociology as well as a foundation
> for more specialized study in the field. Emphasis in this
> class will be placed on basic sociological concepts, the
> nature of the sociological perspective, the logic of social
> inquiry, and recurrent theoretical and methodological prob-
> lems of the discipline. In addition, some of the more
> important areas in sociology will be surveyed.

It then goes on to enumerate a few of these latter. Surely those of us who have studied the history of religious institutions are all too familiar already with this pattern of beginning with orthodox doctrine and only then moving on to seeing how facts are organized into that ideational scheme.

On receiving the letter from Columbia I was bold enough to write back asking why they felt that the modern phenomenologists and structuralists were any more important, interesting, or worthy of a full-scale appointment than other theorists. Van der Leeuw and Lévi-Strauss have come up with some interesting ideas about religion, no doubt; but I asked those at Columbia whether they really regarded them as more illuminating in this realm than, let us say, Hegel and Plotinus—or for that matter, than Samkara. The answer, as might be expected, was that these (at least, the first two) were already covered, under Philosophy of Religion. My point, of course, was that the new writers are theorists of religion in the same sense as were the older ones. Why should the old course not be expanded to cover the new luminaries in the field? I, at least, cannot see how one can do more than (a) study the data; and (b) study interpretations of the data.

What is it that a person knows, who knows structuralism?

I have pondered my own question for a good while, and do not know that I have yet perceived what is going on here. If one asks oneself why Samkara is not included in a Philosophy of Religion course, the answer finally is perhaps that his presuppositions are different from those of the Western student, so that the latter cannot digest, cannot assimilate, his interpretations; merely objectify them. Similarly, if one asks why the phenomenological and structuralist interpretations are not also added to an expanded Philosophy of Religion course, again perhaps the answer is, in somewhat upside-down fashion, that modern students are so indoctrinated as to be unable to digest, to assimilate, Plotinus and Hegel, or Otto or Hocking or Dilthey, these men's orientations being so divergent from their own. (I leave aside contemporary so-called philosophy of religion, of the so-called linguistic or analytic sort, which strikes me as utterly confused, as well as virtually irrelevant to our concerns.) The presuppositions of this modern generation of students are perhaps so firmly utilitarianist, the practitioners are perhaps so oriented to knowing how, not to knowing what, that classical philosophy of religion wanes; and rather than at the interpretation of data, they aim at the teaching of techniques: how to deal with those data, in some sense externally, rather than how to digest them inwardly.

One problem here, in addition to all others, is that for the study of religion—especially other cultures' religion—centrally requisite is a readiness critically to revise one's presuppositions. Few things stand in the way of a genuine awareness of others' religious life more firmly than the imposing of one's own presuppositional categories upon the data of one's observation, ordering the material in terms of one's preformulated conceptual scheme. Surely we all know that. But do we also recognize it here? The methodological presupposition—whatever the method chosen: the sheer presupposition that a given method, especially one thought up by Western intellects, is important—works at least as well as any other *a priori* stance, and indeed better than most, in obstructing one's sensitive perception of what one is studying.

I think that it can be shown that any given method to some degree pre-determines the results that will be got by using it. It is also the case that any given set of preconceptions to some extent pre-determines the results also. Between the two there is, however, a decisive difference. So far as I can see, it is expected that one will be modified, or probably modified, in the course of the inquiry. If we may revert for a moment to that question of generic academic method, that characteristic quality of mind that, so far as I can see, should obtain throughout a university, then may we not insist that a readiness to modify one's pre-convictions must constantly be maintained? Most social scientists have dogmatic presuppositions about the nature of the world, of science, of intellectual truth, and the like, certainly of the supernatural, which are not at issue as they study—especially as they study alien cultures. On the humanities side, I recognize that much is asked of us in the study of religion, in that our most fundamental and precious convictions, whether theological or positivistic, are every day open to revision in the light of what we are studying. I would insist upon this openness as an inescapable qualification for scholarly work. However difficult it be, it would be my observation that humane students of religion are more ready to modify their presuppositions than methodological students are to modify their methodologies, as a result of each new point that they learn in the course of their study or research.

In fact, if I have understood the matter aright, one is actually expected to formulate one's methodological predilections *before* one launches an inquiry. Some years ago I used to serve on selection committees for the joint A.C.L.S.-S.S.R.C. Fellowships for foreign area study. I was struck by the fact that the predisposition was to award fellowships by preference to applicants who had formulated with some exactitude the research project that they were going to India or to the Near East to execute. A well thought out, tightly knit, neatly packaged proposal was expected, and was rewarded. I was much disquieted at this. It is my experience that those persons learn most from especially their first visit to India or the Near East who recognize ahead of time that they do not yet know the best questions to ask; that more than half the point of their trip is to ascertain what is worth investigating, how to formulate one's queries, how to modify one's preconceptions, and the like. Sensitivity, openness, creative response to new awareness, are inimical, so far as I can discern, to the pre-articulated methodological neatness, Western-derived and Western-controlled, that wins the heart of the methodological school.

Let me move to another level of discourse, and speculate as to whether, just conceivably, our problem, or much of it, may not be summed up in the notion of transcendence. I use that term more or less literally, to refer to that which transcends—transcends us, our grasp, our definitions, among other things. Now my suggestion is that maybe it is relevant to our concerns that the modern intellect has tended to deny transcendence, and therefore to stultify itself. Of course, specifically in the study of religion an openness to transcendence might be thought to be the inescapable prerequisite. I am speaking not solely or even primarily about the study of religion, however; and certainly am speaking about an openness not to the *idea* of transcendence, but rather to transcendence itself—and in the first instance, to the transcendence of reality over the known. The interest in epistemology, method, and disciplinary control is in some measure a confining of the intellect to what is already known, or is about to be known, and therefore to ideas, and grows out of a failure to recognize that the proper object of our intellect is something that transcends our knowledge: namely, the real world. We must have the courage to recognize that in the university, as in all true intellectual inquiry, we are oriented to a transcendent reality, which is simply reality itself. If we are not more concerned with our subject-matter, which we do not know, than with our methods, which we do, we have ceased to be true inquirers. (When I say that we do not know our subject-matter, I mean of course that we do not know it except partially, inadequately.)

I personally am a realist as to the past. There are historians, and philosophers, who feel (not merely think, but feel) that the past is not real. ("Where is it?" they ask.) The word "history" originally meant a story about the past; but it has since come to have two quite distinct meanings: namely, the actual course of events in the past, on the one hand, and on the other, an account of those events, written by an historian. The ambiguity between these two can be quite confusing; I solve it simply by using the word "historiography" for the latter. The growing tendency for the word "history" to denote "historiography" rather than a transcendent reality, actuality (not in the French sense), which always eludes our grasp but nonetheless is always the focus of our intellectual attention; that tendency is, to me, alarming. The theoretical history in men's minds is always derivative from, less important than, to be tested against, thought of *always* in subordinate relation to, the real history that actually took place.

The University of Chicago uses the term "History of Religions" to designate an academic discipline. Now for the work of that school, brilliant, profound, exciting, of course I have enormous respect. Yet in this particular terminological matter (and perhaps in the end not solely terminological), I have so strong a sense of the sacredness of the actual, the sheer overpowering majesty of the reality of *was wesentlich geschehen ist*, that I find that Chicago usage almost to have echoes that might be called blasphemous, if you will allow me to confess this. To teach or to study historiography rather than to focus on history as something "out there" is to surrender. I personally speak of the history of religion in the singular, as that to a study of which I am giving my scholarly life; but I recognize that there has also been, intertwined with that, a history of what men call the religions. Yet whether plural or singular, it is vastly greater, more complicated, more subtle, more variegated, more vast than our knowledge of it either is or ever will be. Yet it is there, the final arbiter and criterion and goal of all our inquiry.

Is it, then, that the fundamental problem is simply that we are, and should recognize that we are, studying what is greater than we. In the natural sciences, this is perhaps not quite so. In some sense, the mind of a scientist is greater than all the galaxies together. In the humanities, however, and for that matter in the social sciences, the subject-matter is greater than the student. It is blasphemous to deny this or to ignore it; it is intellectually an error not to recognize it; it is morally wrong to wish that it were not so. We must recognize, accept, and deal with this over-riding fact.

I am haunted by the sense that method, technique, is a device for dominating. The relation between science and technology suggests that if we learn the right method, we can manipulate, control, exert our superiority. If there be any of that in the humanities, we are doomed as scholars. Our task is not to dominate, but to revere; to learn to revere. I return to that remark already cited: "We cannot engineer our way into the sacred."

Let me repeat what I said above: that the best scientists are not technicians, but profoundly human; reverent in the face of an awesomely given universe. Although I said that the human mind is greater than all the galaxies, yet it is also true that a simple stone transcends all human knowledge of that stone.

The word "scholasticism" originally designated the thought in mediaeval Europe of the Schoolmen, the most sophisticated intellectual system of the time. Presently, however, it became a derogatory term, when in course of time that intellectual system became more interested in itself than in the objective world; more interested in ideas than in reality; more concerned with its own procedures and techniques and answers and questions, than in the real world outside. My feeling is that the modern academic enterprise has already entered its own scholastic phase, in this pejorative sense. The interest in methodology seems a kind of narcississtic and self-destructive introversion: the paying of primary attention not to the world around us, but to our ideas about that world.

But enough of my contention that a true appreciation of what we are endeavouring to study requires of us a stress on something other than method. Let me turn to touch briefly on two practical ramifications in the academy. I think them important, but on them we shall not here spend time.

The first is a question as to whether the emphasis on specificity of method is not in danger also of being involved in the sad fragmenting of the university. Did Clarke Kerr's notion of a multiversity not in part have to do with the vision of divergent academic methods separating one division from another, each performing then a different task? "Disciplines" separated from each other by method tend to become separated from each other also in intent (not to mention in jargon); and community is fragmented. I believe profoundly that truth is ultimately one; just as I believe, equally profoundly, that man is ultimately one. I certainly believe that the university is one; and we must strive with might and main to preserve that. The community of scholars, an ideal to which I certainly adhere, is a community of inquirers all bound together by a common devotion to a single purpose, executed in a single way: that of pursuing the truth of the world around us, in open, rational, empirical inquiry. We have a division of labour, each group of us having selected a certain sector of that world to examine. The sector divisions are far from watertight, however; overlaps keep constantly being noted, and regularly prove rewarding. It is important that on principle we recognize no monopolies. Also, we report each our results to the whole.

Secondly, with the new outlook, the university is in danger of disruption horizontally as well as vertically, as student uprisings have brought painfully home to us all. If we teach only techniques, if we offer only what is called "training," if we proffer only methods of attaining something that the students presumably already know that they want, then of course those students should and will decide what they wish to know, to do, what skills they shall select; and in effect then they employ the experts, to satisfy these aspirations. They *use* the university, for their own purposes. We intellectuals become their servants (or at best, those of society, of government), to carry out others' intentions. They are hiring us to provide them with "qualifications," as the modern phrase has it, or "skills," as it also has it, or "tools"; to pursue goals that they have already determined (or, have had determined; or, that they choose irrationally, uncritically).

As scholars, surely we refuse to be used.

As scholars in the humanities, surely we refuse to apply reason only to means, not to ends—and to teach such application.

This brings us then to my final point. To close, I turn from what is known, to the knower. Thus far, apart from these practical moral considerations, I have confessed to you primarily my unease lest the stress on method distort our knowledge; and especially in the humane field, because of the nature of our subject-matter, which is human, and the religious quality of the human at that. There appear to be disquieting implications also, however, on the side not only of the object of knowledge but of the subject—who is human also. Let us in conclusion look more explicitly at that. Are the concept of methodology and the accent on method not in danger of involving an inadequate appreciation of man as learner? To me they seem inherently to underestimate what happens, or can happen, should happen, to the student or scholar in the process of inquiry.

As we have just remarked, they imply that one knows ahead of time what one wants; and has only to find out how to get it. The principle of humane learning, in contrast, is that one discovers in the course of one's study what one is after; what is worth wanting; what one "wants" in the old-fashioned literal sense of what is wanting in one's present state of becoming. To that matter of "becoming" we shall return in a moment; meanwhile let me emphasize that in principle it is possible to learn a method, and even to apply it, without ceasing to be basically what one was before: to come out of the learning process fundamentally the same kind of person as one went into it. A sorry conception, surely!

Humane learning is not a methodological system for gratifying desires, however worthy. It is an exploration of what man as such is; what he has been; what he may be. Or shall we not, rather, say: of what we men have been, may be, and we women; and thereby what we men and women truly, ultimately, are. The individual who enters upon it is therefore exposing his actual self to his potential self; is participating in that process of self-transcendence in which being human in part consists.

For to study man is to study oneself, even when one person studies another (or one society another) separated by much space, or time, or both. What great men and women have produced makes available to us lesser men and women a vision by which we overcome, in part, our lessness. There are facets of our common humanity that lie dormant in most of us until awakened by our coming into touch with others' attainments.

To study a great poem, or a great work of art, or a great idea, is to become more fully human.

And not only what is great can serve us thus. I still hold that there is merit in studying chiefly what men and civilizations have chiefly prized. Yet one can enhance one's vision, one's understanding of oneself, of man, of the universe, can enhance one's humanity, by coming into genuine intellectual apprehension of all men, whatever; great or small. Difference is educative, as well as greatness. And vice, as well as virtue. To study human wickedness is to hold up a mirror to oneself. The aberrations as well as the achievements of our race are eloquent of our own finite infinitude. And the bizarre helps one to understand more truly one's own everyday, what had until now seemed normal.

Our field, of course, marvellously combines difference and greatness. In studying the history of religion we stretch our imagination and our souls by coming to know what is most radically different from that with which we are familiar, at the same time as coming to know what most men perceive as surpassingly great.

Yet by "to know" here is meant something incompatible, surely, with the notion of knowledge as a tool, as though it were external to oneself, were not integrated into the very core of one's being. Methods, so far as they are systematized in formal methodologies, not only are, but I guess are calculated to be, separable from the person who employs them. Let us not in the humanities, surely, be party to the current movement in our society towards depersonalization, including in this case the depersonalization of knowledge. To know is to become. This is one reason why to know the truth is so cosmically important, as well as recognizing that we shall never know it (this side the grave) except partially, inadequately. Yet, I repeat: to know is to become. The point of learning about the natural world is the joy (and virtue) of knowing, and/or the resultant ability to change that world. The point of learning about man is the joy of knowing, which inherently comprises a changing of oneself.

The knowledge that we seek becomes a part of ourselves, and constitutes a transformation—even the knowledge of the multiplication tables in arithmetic, let alone a knowledge of the fall of the Roman empire, let alone a knowledge, and understanding, of an African animist's relation to a fetish, or a Hindu's vision of eternity.

Well, there you have my position—or at least as much of it as I have been able, with immense difficulty and trepidation and inadequacy, and with apologies for this last, to articulate for our discussion. As you see, it is a radical and drastic one; and as you also see, I feel strongly about it. I beg of you: please show me my fallacy. Obviously, the position must be wrong, even though my own mind impels me to it; for better minds than mine seem to see things differently. Persons of greater erudition, intelligence, and wisdom than I are methodologists; though they appear to have ignored—or to have soared above—my particular qualms, which is why I have come here to this conference. I hope that I have sufficiently elucidated my stand and made my reservations sufficiently clear, that you can see where I have gone wrong and can enable me too to see it. Certainly I very much hope that I am wrong. It would be enormously sad if the drift of modern intellectuality, the construction of a new orthodoxy, were as off the track as it seems to me to be. I should be very grateful, therefore, if you can quiet my forebodings.

DISCUSSION

Baird—If I understand correctly, one of your objections to the concern with methodology is that it tends to emphasize the universal and tends to ignore the particular and concrete. Is there not a sense, however, in which the approach that you have given us this evening as an alternative is based on a general theory of human nature? Let me just mention a couple of places here to indicate what I mean.

For example, the statement, "For it so happens that human beings are that kind of creature that cannot in fact be understood unless recognized as human, as personal, and treated humanely. To perceive persons as entities contributing to more rarified theories is inherently to misunderstand those persons and therefore to produce bad theories." Or your distrust of the scholar of Hindus who did not love India. Or perhaps, toward the end, your observation that to study a great poem or great work of art or great idea is to become more fully human. My question simply is: isn't this to a very great extent a general theory of the nature of man, and in that sense does this not put you in the camp with all the rest of us?

Smith—It is a general theory. The former part is based on observation and can be readily empirically documented, I think. But I am not against general theories. I am against the use of the word "methodology" to mean ideology. I'm a bit of a purist on that. I think it's silly to use the word methodology if it has nothing to do with method.

Penner—Can we have a definition of that please?

Smith—Method?

Penner—No, ideology.

Smith—In the paper I used . . . conceptual framework, preconception, ideational stance, preconceived position, or *Weltanschauung*. The concepts that underlie any given study or method or observation seem to me of great importance, and I said in it that this seems to me to be of great significance. But that I don't call methodology . . . .

I think, . . . a chemist has every right to tell a chemistry student that a sophisticated scientific notion of chemistry demands such and such a theory of chemical procedures. But I, as a teacher in the history of religion, cannot say to a Muslim student who comes into my class, for instance, "I have studied history of religion for 40 years or something, and you are Muslim and have this or that ideological framework; chuck it, you've got to learn it my way because I know more about it than you do . . . ." He has as much right to his Islamic *Weltanschauung* as I have to any theory I may have. What I do demand of him is that he be willing to modify his conceptual *Weltanschauung* in the light of new evidence . . . .

But that's not method to my mind . . . . I know that some people call methodological what I call theoretical, preconceptual, whatever.

Question[1] —Prof. Smith, could you amplify that "plus" that the humanistic scholar has that goes beyond what the multi-disciplinary approach might achieve . . . .

You mentioned he used methods of numismatics, art historical approach, psychological approach . . . . On the one hand you seem to be criticizing the multi-disciplinary approach. And yet you do say, if I understand you correctly, that the humane scholar did, by a kind of intuition, what the multi-disciplinary approach is doing in any case. Obviously there must be some "plus" in the humane scholar that wins your approval for him but not for the multi-disciplinary scholar.

Smith—Well, the point there is the question: how does a single scholar's many-faceted approach to a particular thing differ from a multi-disciplinary approach to it? The point there is that a member of a given discipline said to me, "I know that I leave out something. But since I know that my method can't cope with that I leave it out cheerfully." Now if you bring 50 people into the room, each of whom is happy, willing, content to omit something, you have no guarantee at all that it may not be the same thing that all 50 of them are leaving out. The difference with the humanist is that, where he of course leaves things out too, he is not happy about it . . . . He sets out to modify his pre-conceptions or his method or his ideas or something. He is restless until he is able to include that thing in his understanding. That's absolutely crucial . . . . All the social scientists, as far as I can see, or at least the behavioural scientists, acquiesce in the fact that they know they haven't understood anything fully. And that I think is just disquieting.

Question—Prof. Smith, I think I agree with you that, both in terms of the history of the field and the current situation, you can't unify the study of religion in terms of a method . . . . Can you unify the study of religion in terms of subject matter any more than you can in terms of discipline?

Smith—Well, in a sense my answer is mostly yes. It [the subject matter] is given, but not fully . . . .

I have been very restless with the idea of defining religion or indeed defining anything else before you set out. And I thought to myself, if I'm insisting on the subject matter rather than the discipline making our work distinctive, do we not have to define religion. And I've finally solved that one but it added about six pages to my talk so I decided to omit it. But in a sentence, . . . I have finally come up with a definition of religion that I am prepared to stand by: namely, that the religious is that which has been called religious in the Western world, chiefly Christian and Jewish matters, and anything else on earth that can be shown to be comparable.

I'm quite serious about that. It's a Western word, and I disagree, if I may be allowed to, with Prof. Baird on this point, that a scholar has the right to define his terms any way he likes. Both religion itself and even the notion religion are in the hands of religious people, and we cannot define it at our pleasure . . . .

But if you ask, does one have to know what is religious, then, before one sets out to study, the answer is, I think, no. I don't *know*. Certainly I have a hunch as to what the religious is before I study it, but that always turns out rather delightfully to have been partially wrong. And I discover what is religious in the history of the world in the process of studying it. I keep changing my ideas. But still, it is not so unguided as all that. I start with the Christians and Jews and the Hindus and Muslims and Buddhists; that's pretty good to start with. And then as you work at it you find you have to keep refining and modifying and including this and leaving out that and all kinds of things, and other people will criticize you for doing it and you learn from that and so forth. It's a constant process . . . .

Question—How do you know those are the places to look to find it?

Smith—Well, I just start on the question as it is given. After all, we inherit these things. The word comes to us from Western culture, so, nobody would deny, would he, that the Christian and Jewish phenomena are part of our subject matter, and I don't see that one would either for Islamic. Hindu, of course, is tricky. But there's a body of received opinion and it's open to revision. If you can persuade me that any given thing was included and should not have been, . . . or that a given thing is not included and should be, then fine.

Question—Well, you mention that after you study the material you find it is not always what you expected it to be. In other words, what you thought was religious beforehand may not prove to be, or what was not religious might prove to be. But how could such a statement be made unless you have a preconception of what religion is essentially in order to understand what is religious or not?

Smith—Well, I have a hunch ahead of time, but I modify it in the course of the study. And so does everybody else. I mean, I'm not alone—we work together on this. And I probably am not seeing your point.

Baird—I believe that what he's after is the criterion whereby you determine that that which you previously thought was religious is now not so, and the criterion by which you decide that something you previously thought was not, now is, so that that too may not become a hunch.

Smith—Well, in the course of studying, I simply discover that some things that seemed similar are less similar than they appeared to be, and other things that seemed dissimilar are more alike.

Baird—Would that mean therefore that the criterion for including or excluding cannot simply be similarity with something else?

Smith—[It would be similarity] with what I started from.

Question—Which is the Western religious tradition?

Smith—That's right.

Question—Isn't that a method?

Smith—It's a method, but I don't think it's terribly important—I would guess that lots of you could think up better ones. I was asked on this, so that's the way I go. But I don't think that everybody else ought to agree with me on that point. If I come up with something useful on this, something persuasive, then good.

Neusner—. . . . Let me say what I conceive of as method and methodology, since you haven't said what you conceive of it, and I can then offer a definition and you can knock it down.

At the present point in my work I am concentrating primarily on certain literary problems which are going to yield and which already are yielding, for me, interesting insights into religion. And these are texts which I need to analyze and come to understand.

I can't come to this text without a set of questions and things I want to do with them, questions which derive also from a rather long, classical tradition of exegesis as well, which I am trying to augment. These questions and procedures are what I would call method. Now it is true, I share your pragmatism and your suspicion of abstraction, though I don't regard it as a virtue. It is true that I will work within my texts and struggle with them for quite some time and get some results. After a while I find myself asking the same questions relatively systematically and coming up with fairly coherent results so I can even predict where I'm going to be. At the point at which I can state what I'm doing abstractly, I can tell someone else what these methods are about. Now, when I offer these things to colleagues, primarily in an oral way—I wouldn't write these things—and I say, well, look: these are the things I'm doing and why, and they can then at a higher level of abstraction compare them to the work of other people and analyze them from what I would regard as a deeper angle or vision—that would seem to me to be what methodology is about. This helps me very very much.

But if I were to come to my texts with nothing but the text, what's going to come out of it? What's my purpose? What do I want to know about it? Now I think what differentiates Western scholarship from traditional scholarship *is* this very sense of consciousness of doing something while you're doing it. These are the things which I understand as method and methodology, and I am very much for them.

Smith—Certainly one comes to . . . texts with questions. I would guess, I may be wrong, that you always find, while reading texts, some other things that you hadn't thought of asking . . . . Then you say you explain to your colleague what you're doing, how you're doing it; and he elaborates, and so on . . . . This is fine, too, but then what he is doing is writing a history or part of a history of later 20th-century thought in the United States. You're writing history of 16 centuries ago in Palestine. That's fine. Both are quite interesting.

Now, I would regard the latter, the self-consciousness bit, [as something] I'm enormously excited about. I think the becoming self-conscious in the religious field is really what's happening today on earth in the history of religion. For the first time we're on the verge of becoming self-conscious, self-consciously religious (critically, analytically, knowing what we're doing) and this is enormously exciting.

Scharlemann[2] —It is still unclear what is thought of by Prof. Smith as method. So could I pose an illustration . . . . Supposing I would want to find out what the different horizons are . . . . One of the means [by which] I would have to do that is to set up a series of questions on the basis of the text which they answer, and then to determine which of the kinds of answers they give is relatively more basic, until I reach the kind of answer which is self-evident and therefore arrive at a justification. By a technique like that I might be able to discover what the presuppositions, limits or horizons are . . . .

Smith—I'm not against method; I'm sorry if I gave that impression. I don't think one can do anything without doing it in some fashion. And I'm certainly not against being rigorous, systematic, critical, and so on.

What I'm against is putting great *emphasis* on it. Sure, if you are studying any thinker of another age or culture . . . you may devise, you'll have to devise, some way or method for arriving at a result. Having done so, it is the result that is interesting for the rest of us. And it is putting emphasis on the method that troubles me. You should try presumably to persuade us that the result at which you've arrived is one at which the rest of us should also arrive. So unless your argument is cogent, you won't succeed . . . . But if you proclaim this particular method as something that the rest of us should follow or that your students should follow, . . . when presumably the interesting and important thing you've discovered is something about that thinker . . . .

Question—I think the rest of us would agree with that, but then I don't see how the rest of your paper would follow.

Smith—Well, I made this point about scholasticism: I'm really serious about that. For one thing—I don't know if you agree—it seems to me the modern university is in very serious trouble. I lived through the 1969 uprisings at Harvard, and once I had recovered from the sheer weariness of it, in thinking about it, it seemed that this was no minor matter. For centuries we have been admired, the intellectuals, the universities, and so on. We've carried an enormously precious tradition in Western culture. Nowadays the university is under severe attack—and not entirely wrongly. These students had a point. And something, possibly at least, has gone seriously wrong with our whole enterprise. Are you all complacent about universities? Are we not possibly in very, very serious trouble? . . .

Now, the scholasticism business is that it strikes me that we have become more interested in our own ideas than the real world. You can't be an intellectual without being interested in ideas, and even in words . . . . But, unless we can manage to keep that always subordinate to our main purpose, which is outside of us, I think we're in deep trouble.

Penner—. . . I don't understand what it is that prompts [Prof. Smith] to call us ideologists. And let me see if I can get this right. If I understand you correctly, what you're saying is, that somehow the methodologies come to real formulations of something (which I don't agree with, by the way). I think the history of science, and the study of religion as well, have shown us very well that methods have been discarded. The very fact of critical analysis has shown us that some methods have gone by the way. Now [some methods] have gone by the way because a methodology is only an application of a theory, if I understand you correctly. So I would agree with you: there is nothing absolute about method. There is nothing absolute about theory either. The test of the method is: does it somehow verify for us the theoretical framework we are using to understand, describe, and explain religion.

Now, if that's on the track of your paper, then it would seem to me, Prof. Smith, where we may have disagreement, is the theoretical framework you're working with. You may disagree with the theoretical framework of other people because throughout your paper, it is heavily personalist. That is, I think the theoretical supposition of this paper is that we should somehow approach religion from a personal, concrete, particular point of view. Therefore, I would say you would have a method in your work, in your writings, and in your teachings, that approaches religion from that theoretical point of view . . . .

Smith—. . . I obviously have a theory. And I sometimes wonder if the theory is more valuable than other theories it differs from . . . . In these latter days as I grow older I think I probably shall write some theoretical books rather than descriptive historical ones. But heaven knows, theories come and go; and I guess I don't believe that theories encapsulate truth very much . . . . My starting point is, you must not treat human beings as objects, that the relation among human beings is very delicate, very special, very subtle, very problematic, and so on. I presume we all agree on this. Now given that fact, what are the intellectual and academic and procedural, if you like, implications of that fact? Well, I'm trying to work it out—and I don't fancy that I shall come up with any great theories on the matter—but even if I did it wouldn't help. The point is to recognize what is actually there.

I guess I do feel that for, say, Christians to understand Hindus, or for positivists to understand Muslims, or Muslims to understand Buddhists and the like, is an enormously difficult matter. And if you really want to do it, which, I take it, is the comparative religionist's aspiration, you first of all have to . . . respect the people you're looking at . . . .

II

THE STUDY OF RELIGION AS THE STUDY OF TRADITION IN JUDAISM

Jacob Neusner

To begin, let me choose among available definitions of "religion." I find congenial the one offered by Van A. Harvey,

> A religion . . . may be regarded as a perspective, a standpoint, in which certain dominant images are used by its adherents to orient themselves to the present and the future . . . a way of looking at experience as a whole . . . a way of interpreting certain elemental features of human existence.[1]

I find this definition congenial because it lays stress, as Harvey's context requires, on the cultural aspect of religion, making room for the collective imagination as well as for the present moment. For Judaism, the cultural, the societal, and the historical constitute primary and formative categories. No definition of religion which fails to stress these aspects of religious phenomena is going to suffice.

Yet the intellectual, individual, and immediate, or contemporary, side to the religious life cannot be left out. When we consider the central religious experiences of Judaism, we find the definition of the faith in terms of tradition, but tradition understood as paradigmatic experience, perceived to be vivid and very present. That is to say, experience of the perfect and eternal, lived in the here and now, joined to the myth which describes and reshapes ordinary life in the model of that experience of eternity or of the sacred, together constitute tradition. The Passover *Haggadah*, which, after all, is simply an exegetical exercise in the Deuteronomic conception of Israel's life, makes that fact explicit. "*We* were slaves of Pharaoh in Egypt." The stress is on those present, not on some long-dead ancestors. "If God had not brought our fathers forth from Egypt, then surely we, and our children, would be enslaved . . ." The generations are three: our fathers, we, and our children—immediate past, present, and immediate future, in accord with the perceptions of living people, for whom great-grandparents and great-grandchildren are scarcely a reality. This then is underlined in the parable of the four sons, which begins with the wicked one, who asks,

> What is all this drudgery of yours for?

And the narrative proceeds,

> Mark the words and the tone, "This drudgery of yours," as if he were not one of us.

> Answer him in the spirit of his question, "All this I do because of what God did for me—for me, not for you."

And there follows,

> This is the promise which stood by our forefathers and stands by us, for neither once, nor twice, nor three times was destruction planned for us. In every generation God delivers us from their hands.

And at the end,

> For ever after, in every generation, everyone must think of himself as having gone forth from Egypt, for we read in the Torah, "In that day thou shalt teach thy son, saying, All this is because of what God did for me when I went forth from Egypt." It was not only our forefathers that the Holy One . . . redeemed. Us too, the living, he redeemed together with them . . .

These passages could be duplicated, in one form or another, throughout the religious experience of Judaism, and the counterpart of their spirit is to be discerned in the secular writings of contemporary Jews as well. They show that a religious tradition, claimed to be among the more historical traditions, also exemplifies the vivid contemporaneity of tradition, the capacity of tradition not solely to preserve dead experience, but to shape and endow with meaning ordinary everyday life in the present. We err in regarding Judaism as primarily cultural, societal, and historical—traditional—in its focus. So far as Judaism is a living faith, it is personal, mythical, or intellectual (in a broad sense), and acutely contemporary.

Yet what is important to the historian of religion in the Judaic religious life is the stress on tradition, and what is distinctive in the study of Judaism is what it teaches us about the study of traditions as an aspect or mode of the study of religions. Let me now define what I do not mean by tradition. I do not mean by tradition, "Something which is handed on intact from one generation to the next." I do mean, "something handed on from the past which is made contemporary and transmitted because of its intense contemporaneity." Tradition involves both the giver and the taker, backward in time and forward as well. It imposes a dynamic relationship, a creative tension, between the remote past, with its authority based on a myth of revelation, as we shall see below, and the remote future, with its power vested in the capacity to continue to vivify, or to abandon and thus kill, the received legacy. Let me give two examples of what I mean by tradition.

The first derives from a just completed research of mine on Eliezer ben Hyrcanus, a 1st-century rabbi. What I found, as I dissected traditions, or authoritative sayings, attributed to Eliezer in accord with the later generations' references to what he was alleged to have said, is that the several strata of tradition were strikingly interrelated. If an early follower of Eliezer alleged that he gave a ruling, a later tradent—one who participates in the formation and transmission of tradition—would likely do one of two things. Either he would refine the substance of that ruling, or he would hand on in Eliezer's name a ruling either spun out of the principle established in the original saying or closely related to it. I found out that it would be highly unlikely that to Eliezer would be attributed a saying with no roots whatever in the primary and original corpus of teachings assigned to him by the circle of his contemporaries and disciples. That seemed to me an unexpected result, an example of how disciplined and principled was the formative process of tradition. So by "tradition" in this sense we may understand, the developing out of the teachings of an early authority the logical principles, and, from them, the necessary consequences for later times. Tradition in this sense is living, yet, as I said, accurate and careful, mindful of what has gone before. It is not capricious, not subjective, not ahistorical, not indifferent to the facts of the past.

My second example is drawn from a story about how a major authority served a meal to his underlings. One version of the story justifies this action as follows:

> The Holy One . . . causes the winds to blow and clouds to
> ascend and rain to descend . . . and prepares a table before
> every single person, and as regards ourselves, should not

> Rabban Gamaliel [patriarch of his day] . . . stand and serve
> drinks to us [b. Qid. 32b].

The other version reads:

> The Holy One . . . gives to everyone according to his needs
> . . . and not to fit men and righteous only, but even to the
> wicked, worshippers of idols. Concerning Rabban Gamaliel,
> how much the more so is it fitting that he stand and serve
> drinks to sages and sons of Torah [Mekhilta Amalek,
> Horovitz-Rabin pp. 195-6].

What is striking is that the first version stresses that God serves man, so the authority serves *his* servants in the model of God. The second, by contrast, says that since God serves the fit and the unfit, so all the more should Gamaliel serve masters of Torah and sages, who alone are *fit*. This is an example of how a tradition not only is carried on, but also may be made to serve the theological and polemical needs of a later generation. In this case, a fairly standard story about divine beneficence is turned into an apologetic for the authority of the rabbis, even over their own leader. The story is made to state that serving the rabbis is an act in imitation of God. In the first instance, we are told that just as God serves the world, so the patriarch, Gamaliel, should serve the world. In the second, a drastic revision has God both serve the righteous and the wicked, so Gamaliel, the patriarch, at the very least should serve the sages—a very different message. I tend to think the first story is the earlier one, and to find the differences in the second evidences of revision, at a later point, in behalf of an important Rabbinical polemic.

As we noted, tradition involves both the giver and the   taker. What the literary instance just given shows is how the tradition proves vital, serviceable for polemic and thus for the discussion of contemporary issues, long after its original theme and form are established. The "giver" here is the story-teller who has handed on a little *pericope* about how the patriarch, in serving his guests, imitates God, who serves nature. The "taker"—the one who revised the story—then has turned the story into something relevant to his particular and distinctive concerns. Tradition as process of handing on and passing forward thus is dynamic and not static. Its interest is not in what was originally said alone, but in how what was said in the past endows with meaning, imposes sense upon, the issues of the new age. Tradition is killed when handed on unchanged. It is vivified when it goes forward, while not intact, fundamentally unimpaired.

These two examples of a living tradition tell us a great deal about the study of Judaism as the study of traditions and their history.

First, we learn that the study of Judaism involves the study of literary materials, by contrast to the study of living liturgy, with its gestures and symbols, processionals and music, which enjoys vividness without encapsulation in words. The study of Judaism requires a wider focus than is commonplace for the study of theology, with its stress on abstract theological ideas, and with its imperfect capacity to come to grips with those ideas which do not yield abstraction, with the substance of myth or of law, for example.

Second, we learn that the study of Judaism involves reflection, in particular, on the sayings and stories of men who were important legal authorities (for the issue in the story of Gamaliel is whether it is proper to do such-and-so). So the focus of the tradition is not on indiscriminate materials which have been handed down, but on a very particular type of information, sayings and stories about what people are supposed to do.

Third, we learn that the study of Judaism involves the study of the *history* of traditions, for it is clear that in the transformation of materials—their interpretation in later times, their revision in terms of the interests of later generations—we are going to locate the essential traits of the tradition as process. That is to say, if you want to know about Judaism, you had better ask not about its condition at a given point in its history (especially not about its condition in contemporary times), but rather about its dynamics, its continuing processes, its "progress" through time. To learn what is distinctive about Judaism one will want to ask about those permanent traits and trends which, from age to age, turn out to speak to and for the accumulated tradition, on the one side, and also to and for the living generation, on the other.

The examples I offered of the vital tradition teach two facts. First, as I stressed, the tradition is not capricious, does not assign, without grounds or reasons, a saying to an ancient authority, merely because a living person would find it useful for that ancient authority to have stated such a saying. Second, the tradition does make room, through the processes of retelling and reinterpreting the tradition, for the most current concerns. The "rabbinization" of the story about Gamaliel, the intrusion of "rabbis" and "sages" where the original account knew nothing except about nature and "all mankind," shows us how a story might be reworked for the theological interests of its tellers.

Now one question is deeply inappropriate for the study of such traditions, and that is, did this story really take place? The intense concern to locate the actual words of a given authority, to be able to make a determination of whether or not something really happened, commits outrage upon the materials of a tradition. For those materials to begin with do not allege concerning themselves the sort of historical interest, let alone historical accuracy, implicit in such a question. The contrary is the case. When we tell of what a great authority said or did, we speak of eternities and of the sacred. We mean to say, This is how holy things *are*, not how, once and for a single, finite moment, they were. The point and purpose of tradition is not to pass on historical facts, but both to create and to interpret contemporary reality, to intervene in history. The tradents' interest in the past is solely because of its paradigmatic value, not for its authority over the present in some lesser, banal and factual sense. The past is not dead, is not past, specifically because it is paradigmatic.

But if the past is paradigmatic, then the past is perceived not as "historical" but as very present. Then what of the claim that Judaism (or Christianity, or Islam) is a "historical religion"? I think what has been meant is this: Judaism is not a religion of myth, a religion which tells stories about things which did not actually happen, but which recounts events which really did take place. Why should that claim be important? I think it was important to historicistic theology, which proposes to replace matters of "faith" with statements of "historical fact," so to solve the crisis of conviction confronting 19th- and 20th-century Jews. By claiming that Judaism (among other allegedly historical religions) did not deal in faith but in facts, the challenge of positivism would be met—by complete surrender. But I argue that that theological statement about Judaism as a "historical religion" is simply false on the face of it, leading to a profound misinterpretation of the meaning of "being Jewish." And the historicistic theory of authority misinterprets the theory of authority behind tradition in Judaism, as we shall observe shortly.

So far as we ask about the traits and definition of a religious tradition, therefore, we want to know about the process and perspective, the standpoint and dominant images, used by adherents to orient themselves to the present and future. That inquiry is the opposite of the historical one. True, to gain an accurate picture of the way in which a tradition works, of its dynamism, we have to ask many historical questions. But these questions are not properly framed solely in terms of whether the tradition is "true," with truth measured by historical verifiability. Rather we want to know whether and how tradition changes, and the way these changes reveal what is taking place in the imagination of the people who took up the tradition and turned it into the center of their being. Tradition serves as the mode of orientation toward the present and future, as the way of interpreting existence, not because it tells us where we have been, but because it explains who we are, what we are, where we are, and whither we should go.

Let me return to the living "tradition" of the Passover *Haggadah*, which I introduced at the outset. The stress is that "we were slaves and now are free." God saved and saves *us*, not them, the dead, alone. The son who asks, "What is this to you?" is wicked. But what makes the ritual of the bitter herbs and the unleavened bread, the myth of the Exodus from Egypt, into vivid and intensely meaningful experiences is their perceived correspondence to the contemporary experience of ordinary folk throughout the history of the Jewish people: "Not once nor twice nor three times was destruction planned for us." The experience of a small people, scattered throughout the world, facing in every generation the fact of alienation and differentiation from the rest of society—that experience, whether or not accompanied by oppression and destruction, as in our own day, is made intensely meaningful because the people are able to see themselves as reliving what has long passed. They therefore are able to seek for themselves the redemption which, they hope and believe, is just as permanent, just as formative and paradigmatic, as is the experience of alienation and oppression. People are able to see themselves as having gone forth from Egypt because they know in their everyday life what it means to be "slaves to Pharaoh in Egypt." The universality of that experience, the omnipresence of the yearning for the passage "from slavery to freedom, from anguish to joy, from mourning to gladness, from darkness to light" is shown by the capacity of these same images to embody the experience of so many other peoples.

The historian of religion differs from the historian, therefore, in his study of traditions. He asks a quite separate set of questions. His inquiries, in my view, are more appropriate to the nature of his evidence. What he wants to know is not solely whether the Israelites really went forth from Egypt, but what the belief that the Israelites really went forth from Egypt teaches us about the history, culture, and society of the people for whom that fact of life serves as a paradigm and explanation for contemporary reality. The historian of religion treats historical events as utterly contemporary in their meaning, whatever period in the history of the tradition concerns him. He understands that every tradition is a historical fact. Someone told a story. Whether or not the story is so, the telling of the story is itself a tremendous fact, and deserves most serious interpretation. What we know from the telling of the story is a whole set of facts about the mind and imagination of the teller, about the society to whom he told the story, about the cultural realities to which the story was deemed pertinent and which were reflected (one may take for granted) in the details of the story. It is sufficient, therefore, to know the history of a hero—that is, the ways in which his life was narrated and interpreted in times long after his death— without asking whether said hero did and taught what he was supposed to have done.

Let me cite here an extreme example of the gullibility and childishness of the historical hermeneutic. There is a saying in the Talmud, told about Hillel, "One day, walking beside a stream, he saw a skull, and he said, 'Because you drowned others, you were drowned. And those that drowned you will be drowned.'" I need not dwell on the philosophy of this saying. What have the historians done with it? A debate, the participants of which will, mercifully, remain unnamed, raged for some 20 years about the identity of the person whose skull Hillel saw, the day on which Hillel saw the skull, and the events which led up to the person's being drowned. Along the same lines, we have a story that Hillel came up from Babylonia to the land of Israel. This saying is in the context of a comparison of Hillel to Ezra, that is, of Hillel as law-giver. The point is fairly clear. The story tells us that the people who told it saw the founder of their movement as equivalent to Ezra, who revived the life of the community of Jerusalem just as "Hillel"— that is, the later followers of Hillel—proposed to give a new Torah and so refound the life of the community. But a historian figured out that Hillel came up from Babylonia on the 15th of March in the year 30 B.C. and proposed, in all seriousness, that the anniversary of that "event" be celebrated by contemporary Jewry. That is one way in which historians try to serve the mythopoeic function of the ancient story-tellers. The sage's cloak does not fit.

It is the perspective of the history of religions which liberates the sources from the straitjacket of historical studies, narrowly construed, and opens the way to the study and interpretation of traditions in a way congruent to their own purpose and point. For no one in the religious tradition proposed to preserve what happened solely because knowing what happened matters, without attention to its larger and wider meanings. The conviction that raised facts about the past from anti-quarianism to value-forming and society-shaping knowledge is peculiarly Western, and in the main, Protestant. Yet that very concern for the past— for "just what happened"—resulted less in a sympathetic understanding of what had happened, than in an effort either to judge the past or to make use of its facts in the vindication and verification of the contemporary world-view. As A. Leo Oppenheimer states,

> The humanities have never been successful in treating alien civilizations with that tender care and deep respect that such an undertaking demands. Their conceptual tools are geared to integration on their own terms and to assimilation along Western standards.[2]

Anyone who doubts the justice of Oppenheimer's critique of Assyriology pursued by humanists had best read the studies of Judaism carried out by Protestant, Catholic, or Jewish theologians, nearly all of them exercises in theological apologetics in the cloak of historical science and in the guise of scholarship.

The reason, I think, is that historical studies tend to take for granted their original, uncriticized ideological foundations. These are based upon the simple conviction that one must distinguish "whether or not something actually happened, whether it happened in the way it is told or in some other way . . . ."[3] When historians come to non-Western civilizations, they come with a considerable agendum. Assyriology began

> at the moment when Western man was eager to step out of that magic circle, the field of energy that protects, preserves, and confines every civilization . . . . Western man became . . . willing and able to appreciate and to evaluate with objectivity his own civilization, to correlate other civilizations, and to strive for an understanding of some over-all design and plan . . .

That is the point at which not only Assyriology, but the whole range and spectrum of historical sciences, took shape.

This curious concatenation of events in the history of Western consciousness—the concern for what "really" happened, on the one side, and the search for self-consciousness through the inquiry into what happened in other than the known Western and Protestant setting, on the other—stands behind the study of traditions for narrowly historical purposes which goes on today as it has in the past. It accounts, too, for the intense interest in that vexed question, the personality, character, and teaching of the "historical Jesus." For the theologian lacking faith in the Christ of faith, the search, for purely scientific and completely disinterested, objective historical motives, for the historical Jesus seemed a happy way out of the dilemma of preserving an essentially religious heritage in the absence of religious conviction. If it could be shown that the Jesus of history really said such-and-so, then the authority of that saying would be established, taken for granted. Why there should be much difference between a saying believed for 18 centuries to have been said by Jesus and one pronounced as genuine by the authority of historical science was never clearly spelled out. Rather, it was taken for granted that the authority of the saying rested with the authority of the one who said it. If one could show Jesus really said it, then that sufficed. The circle of faith, if broken, could be restored. The authority of Jesus could be taken for granted, if history could show he exerted authority. It was merely a different way of arguing about the effects of that authority—through the transmission of tradition or through the determination of the historian. In other words, the historian who would determine what Jesus really had said, in the assumption that the fact of his having said it made all the difference, is not easily to be distinguished from the theologian. Both take for granted what someone outside the circle of faith does not, namely, that the question is important, the answer somehow determinative, normative, or authoritative.

I do not claim that the task of finding out, as best we can, just what happened is unimportant or secondary. The interpretive task of the historian of religions wholly depends upon the prior accomplishment of the scientific task of the historian. Before we know two things, we cannot interpret anything: first, who told a story, to whom, and under what circumstances; second, whether and in what degree does the story correspond to an actual event. These are narrowly historical questions, and before we know the answers, the heuristic task is premature. For the beginning of interpretation is to know *who* and *what* it is that we are to interpret, whether we have a fantasy, or a fantastic view of reality, or a mundane statement of an everyday event. Every tradition constitutes a historical datum, a fact, and it is for the historian to supply the historian of religions with the description, the facticity, of that fact: its setting, its veracity, above all, to what and to whom it testifies. I am in entire agreement with my colleague, Horst R. Moehring, who states,

> Any historian, whether "just" a historian or a historian of religions, must first of all understand the material with which he is working. The interpretation of an event will have to be determined differently, if critical research shows that it never happened in the way in which it is presupposed in the interpretation.

My criticism of historicism is not to be understood as a rejection of the achievements of historians, but as a complete affirmation of their method and results, together with the warning not to exceed the just limits of those results. It is the historian who makes theological statements, like the biologist who makes philosophical ones, that is here viewed as ludicrous. Both claim to an authority not conferred by the method or results of sound, positivistic inquiry. For both, facts are asked to transcend themselves, information is asked to surpass its intellectual quotient. Let history be history, let theology be theology, and let historians of religion reflect upon both—and more.

Having many times referred to the "authorities" of the Rabbinic tradition and just now criticized the view that historical events are "authoritative," I find it is time to face squarely the issue, What is the nature of the authority of tradition? If, as I claim, merely because something happened, it is not therefore authoritative, then on what basis is "tradition," viewed as suggested here, regarded as "normative"?

We begin with the theologico-mythic answer of Rabbinic Judaism. The "tradition" is normative because it was revealed to Moses at Sinai; the Torah is God's will for Israel, and the contents of the Torah comprehend both the written Scripture everyone knows and the Oral Torah *handed on as tradition* at the same time: "Moses received the Torah from Sinai and handed it on to Joshua . . ." The two key words meaning tradition, QBL, "received," and MSR, "handed on," occur in that weighty sentence. In post-biblical Hebrew, there are two ways of saying tradition, *qabbalah* and *massoret*. The nature of the authority of tradition then is clear: it derives from God's word to Moses, called "our rabbi." Central to the concept of authoritative tradition, specifically of Torah, therefore, is the view of Moses as the authority, the *rabbi*, who stands behind the Pentateuch and the Oral Torah of the later rabbis. To ask, at what point and how does *tradition* become authoritative, therefore, we must ask, when is Pentateuch claimed to be Mosaic? Where does the concept of Moses as the archetypical and prototypical rabbi emerge? Above all, what is the alternative authority, over against that of the tradition of Moses?

E.J. Bickerman recently pointed out[4] that it is with Philo that the Mosaic authorship of the Torah becomes axiomatic. While Moses as author of, and authority behind, Scriptures or sacred revelations occurs earlier, I think it is clear from Bickerman's observation that the authority of Moses becomes important in the Judaism of the last century or so before 70 A.D., and that that importance, specifically, is to Hellenistic Judaism. In the Rabbinic Judaism, taking shape after 70, the figure of Moses similarly is exceedingly important. Yet in the Rabbinic traditions about the Pharisees before 70, Moses occurs in not a single saying, apart from the opening sentence of Avot cited above. Further, the earliest versions of the chain of Pharisaic tradition beginning with that sentence know nothing of Moses, Joshua, elders, and prophets; these are added only in the last chain, which is unlikely to derive from the period before 200 A.D. It is at that same time that the Mishnah itself was promulgated, under the claim that it contains the Oral Torah of Moses, enjoying the same normative and authoritative status as the written Torah, the Pentateuch. The claim that the tradition was handed on orally, through memorization, begins after, and not before 70, and becomes well attested only after 140.

My colleague Horst R. Moehring points out the meaning of these facts, that Mosaic authorship of the Pentateuch is important, first, to Alexandrian Judaism, and, second, to the rabbis after 70, with particular prominence coming after 140. The answer lies in what the two groups—Alexandrian Jews, post-70 rabbis—have in common. It is temporal or spatial distance from the Temple of Jerusalem. While the Temple stood, for Jews living in the land of Israel it was the fount of authority. The reason, however, was its place not merely in the administration of their affairs, but in the shaping of the sacred canopy under which they lived out their days, by the stars of which they navigated the course of life, so to speak. The centrality of the Temple in the mythic life of the people may be shown in many ways. One, just now important in my work, is the view that all forms of purity and impurity are referred ultimately to the Temple, which indicates, as Mary Douglas argues, that that is the point on which the lines of authority, social and cosmic, converge.[5]

It is with the collapse of the Temple as the organizing force of society and ordinary affairs—either because of distance, with the Alexandrians, or because of the unavailability of the cult, after 70, and of the obviously permanent end of the cult, after 140, that we find growing importance attached to the figure of Moses. Moses the mystagogue or the rabbi, for the pre-70 Alexandrians or the post-70 rabbis, respectively, now stands behind tradition, whose authority depends upon its origin with Moses, and with God. Formerly, the Temple cult provided the center of the organization of reality. Now God does, through Moses' Torah. The tradition of things gone by which still endure takes its place.

I therefore offer an entirely historical explanation for the authority of tradition in Rabbinic Judaism, simply by pointing to the time at which the change in the basis of the existence of society and of the interpretation of reality took place. Yet it should not be understood as an essentially historical explanation. For what is important is not the time of the destruction of the Temple. Philo and perhaps some of his predecessors show the physical existence of the Temple is not at issue. What I think is important is a change affecting many groups in Greco-Roman antiquity, where Temples were closing not solely by reason of destruction, where new modes of relating to the divinity were taking shape. As Jonathan Z. Smith observes, it is at that same time that magicians became important; the substance of their magical actions commonly involved an act of sacrifice.

What is the nature of the authority of tradition in Judaism? The answer is first given in the mythico-theological language of Rabbinic Judaism itself, then accounted for the point at which that language became significant. Tradition is authoritative because it comes from Moses, therefore from God, an idea especially important in the century after the destruction of the Temple. The authority of the "authorities" of the Rabbinic tradition rests upon their holding, embodying, and handing on the Torah of Moses, a Torah conceived in God's image. The rabbi therefore stands as the paragon of Moses "our rabbi" who imitated God, his rabbi. The authority of the rabbi is based upon the myth that the rabbi exemplifies God's image, is holy like God. The Temple and the cult exhibit the earthly model of the heavens; the rabbi, priest and mystagogue, carries forward the ancient mode of authority.

What of "Torah" or tradition, within the proposed interpretation? It seems to me clear that "Torah" takes the place of the earthly Temple in the functioning of the Jews' social and political life, on the one hand, and of the cosmic Temple in the articulation of their imaginative world and expression of the sacred on the other. The foundation of the authority of tradition must then be compared to that of the authority of the Temple, a comparison which we cannot fully undertake within the narrow framework of our present problem.

Finally, let us ask about the role of history of religions in the study of tradition. History of religions, with its sympathetic interest in the wide range of religious traditions, with its capacity to recognize the historian-of-religions' own situation, and to take account, in the interpretive task, of the stance of the interpreter himself, has the capacity to turn the study of traditions into something of significance for the study of the larger issues of religion. The reason, as is already clear, is that the historian of religions has the capacity to take seriously and in its own terms the importance of tradition, without asking the reductionist question of whether tradition really is right about the people alleged to have participated in its formation or to have served as the object of its rule or teaching. The accumulation of story, law, wisdom, and theology preserved in the tradition is a rich resource for the understanding and interpretation of the cultural history of a religion, but only when allowed to stand as a fact in itself. For the tradition—its shape, its development, its modulations through time—testifies with unfailing accuracy, as I said, to the mind and imagination of the people who gave and continue to give it that shape, who nurture that development, and who effect those modulations.

This I think is to be taken as fact. But for the historian of religion, the discovery of the people to whose perception of the sacred the tradition *does* testify as a matter of fact does not constitute an end in itself. Once we have located the people who stand behind traditions, unlike historians we have begun, not completed, our work. The historians then tend to reduce the facts, purported to be contained in traditions, to the interests and prejudices of the people who hand on, therefore who stand behind the distortion of, those facts. But the historian of religions is not interested solely or even primarily in what really happened in the period of which the tradition speaks, but rather, in what we learn about the people *to* whom the tradition speaks.

Yet among historians of religion, one notices a curiously limited range of interests. Many scholars of early Christianity bore us by their intense, repetitive interest solely in whether Jesus really said something. Some of them pronounce the bulk of Jewish tradition pertaining to the period as "worthless" because it does not help them recover what Jesus really said or did not say. But historians of religion, I think, exhibit a parallel, if less paralyzing, narrowness of interest, in one sort of religious data, those deriving from studies of symbols. Their definition of religion in some measure may be derived from an examination of what they regard as the worthwhile result of their inquiry. Let me take as an example the late Erwin Goodenough, whom I revere. Goodenough took as his task the interpretation of the symbols found in the archaeological remains of ancient Judaism, and his primary interest—beyond the brilliant scholarship required for his work—lay in the interpretation of the universal appeal or meaning of those symbols. This he found in their salvific symbolism. Virtually every symbol found in ancient Jewish art was shown ultimately to bear salvific valence, to serve as a means of expressing the devotee's yearning for salvation. To establish the correctness of this interpretation, Goodenough therefore had to distinguish between the specific meanings associated with a given symbol in its own setting—that is, the verbal explanation found in the literature referring to such a symbol—and the larger, universal meaning, *not* given verbal explanation but latent in the imagination of anyone exposed to such a symbol, to be located in the parallel appearances of said symbol in other cultures. Consequently, Goodenough took slight interest in the Rabbinic literary data. These, by definition, were adjudged irrelevant to the task of the interpretation of Jewish symbols. He drastically limited the range of his interpretative possibilities, on the one hand, and equally radically limited the range of data with the interpretation of which he would concern himself, on the other. This is what

I mean by a certain narrowness of interest on the part of historians of religion. It derives, obviously in the case of Goodenough, from the sense that part of the task of history of religions is to compare religious data, and from the recognition that the task of comparison must be considerably facilitated by the location of those elements of a given religious tradition which may be freed of their specificities and concrete location in an incomparable setting, a concrete culture.

A religious tradition, however, is not to be limited to its non-verbal aspects, on the one side, or to those myths of such obviously universal significance as to make possible the task of comparison, on the other. It must be taken whole and complete, determinative on its own of what is important and of what is "religious." So far as we take seriously Harvey's stress on religion as a way of interpreting certain elemental features of human existence, we have to understand as *religious* whatever in a given tradition functions as part of such an interpretative enterprise. Accordingly, even the interest in history itself has to be subsumed—even reduced—to its significance in the interpretation of the mind and self-understanding of a given religious community or society, our own. The historical hermeneutic, which assigns importance to something in relationship to whether the historian can persuade himself something has really happened, testifies, after all, to the positivistic hermeneutic of a given setting. Similarly, history of religions needs to take seriously the quintessential, revelatory nature of law in Judaism, or of purity rites in Zoroastrianism, Hinduism, and Judaism, as much as of the structure of the Buddhist Temple, the character of the Islamic creed, or the Christology of the Roman Catholic Church.

All religious data, and not merely those data pertinent to myth and ritual, are to be subjected to the historian of religions' mode of interpretation. It is history of religions which has repeatedly claimed the urgency of preserving the concern for what is religious about religion, without engaging in the reduction of religion to an aspect of history and culture, of psychology and sociology, or of metaphysics and philosophy. Then history of religions has likewise to take seriously the religious meaning of the study of tradition and the results of that study. This is in two aspects. First, place is to be found in the history of religions for the results of those who, like myself, think much of consequence is to be learned from the history of the growth and continuity of a given religious tradition. And, second, place is to be found among data thought worthy of interpretation by history of religions for the fact that, in Judaism at least, the *study* of the tradition itself is an act of profound religious consequence.

DISCUSSION

Question—Prof. Neusner, this distinction you have made between the historian's task and that of the historian of religion is very illuminating, and I am wondering if the distinction doesn't somehow slide over into what has now become the theological or religious function of the historian in our time. Because, the reason that the tradition can serve as a model . . . of reality is that the reality it is a model of was an historical event that justified believing that the world was such and such a way . . . .

Now, does this not suggest that to the extent that the historian can either substantiate or disqualify certain historical events, the foundation for the model for contemporary life now is neither justified nor abandoned? So this means in our own time, when we've passed the era when the model of reality was assumed, the historian has a very important religious function.

Neusner—. . . I think [this] produces exceedingly bad history . . . . And the reason it [has produced] exceedingly bad historical work, at least in the area in which I toil, . . . was that the historians were taking on themselves a range of questions with clearest implications, that (a) they had no business to deal with; and (b) that was obscuring the nature of their evidence.

[The reason is that] if to the formation of Judaism, the question of whether Hillel actually came up from Babylonia on March 15 in the year 30 B.C. is an important question, . . . then the religious Jews, and there are very many, are going to join the argument and the orthodox are going to say it really happened, and they're going to espouse all kinds of "religious" positions on *historical* questions. What difference does it make to religious persons? . . . It shouldn't make any difference . . . . The sources are terrible. If you want to study the historical Hillel, I wouldn't even know how to figure out what really could be attributed to him . . . .

But if we can't allow the historians to do their work free of the theological agendum, then the nature of our evidence is never going to be clear, and there is a sociological and political side, too. I think we will never be able to speak to people we really want to speak to among the Jews—the religious Jews . . . .

Question—Can you really totally divorce the historian and let him work in a theological vacuum and then go accordingly with what he comes up with?

Neusner—. . . Your question is a serious one, and that has to do with what happens when the historian discovers that the event never happened. Well, there's an obvious answer which I'm sure you're familiar with. And that is that the event has taken on a facticity of its own. And that's where I would stand . . . . You ask about the Exodus from Egypt. We are now, if it happened at all, 35 centuries away . . . . Who cares, and who would know, and what kind of evidence would be required to prove it really happened . . . . But I know that at the Seder I had at my house 10 days ago, my wife was profoundly moved by this. . . . Everybody's got a Pharaoh, you see. I can't conceive of anything that could matter less at this point, than discovering an eyewitness account which everybody verifies . . . .

Goldstein[6] —My question is not exactly a question, because I've been the target and the enemy because I come from the enemy camp. After all, I am an historian, and I'd like to make a few observations.

One is, the fundamentalist religion will always be with us. There are fundamentalist Jews and fundamentalist Christians, and to the fundamentalists it matters very very much indeed whether you can prove or disprove whether an event has happened. But, by my standards as an historian, and by Prof. Neusner's standards as an historian, an historian makes a mistake when he writes either for or against fundamentalism. Prof. Neusner makes a very good plea, but I object to his distinguishing historians and historians of religion for *good* history. What is good history? Good history is history which respects the evidence and respects it for what it is. We aren't always aware of what our evidence is. The best historian tries to be the most aware of what the evidence is. And the best historian tries to respect *all* evidence. Zoroastrian scriptures are boring for historians who want to write political history, who want to know who was king and want to know how many wars he fought. And Plucidides established that pattern for historians.

But an historian who is interested in what the evidence can show will find great interest in Zoroastrian scriptures . . . . He will find great interest in the purity law of the Pharisees and rabbis which will show things which people thought at the time. And the Rabbinic stories tell you what the storyteller and his audiences believed. Those are facts of history, and Prof. Neusner pleaded for the respect of the evidence and for using the evidence for what it *can* show. And what we all plead for is *good* history: history of religion, history of anything else should be good history, respecting the evidence and using it for what it can show.

Question—In light of what you have said about the Exodus in response to these questions, is the distinction . . . between a God who reveals himself in history, as in, supposedly, Judaeo-Christian religion, is this *not* a valid distinction to make any longer?

Neusner—. . . Well, I don't find meaningful the distinction between the God who reveals himself in myth and the God who reveals himself in historical events, no. I don't even understand what is being said and why that helps . . . . I think this is a mode of thought which was exceedingly important for the historicist theologians whose day I believe is done . . . .

McCue[7] —I'm trying to get at a certain perspective on the development of positions . . . . As you present matters it almost sounds as though what you label fundamentalism or historicist theology comes about rather uniquely as a reaction to positivism of the 19th century . . . .

Neusner—I have not meant to suggest that the consciousness of history begins in the 19th century, or that Maimonides or Judah Hallevi or, let us say, people in the Talmud, didn't believe that the things really happened, no. I think your phrasing of the matter is . . . exactly correct . . . . What bothers me very deeply is the continuation of this mode, this theological apologetic, . . . into 20th-century Jewish thought, which I regard as impoverished and misguided . . . .

Question—You may have already answered this, but do you feel it's the nature of the content . . . of Judaism which makes the approach of study via tradition-methodology useful, or is this useful across the board? In other words, would this approach be useful in a situation where there wasn't a sense of tradition in the material?

Neusner—I don't know of a situation where you have literary data which are regarded as of religious consequence where there is no sense of tradition in the material. After all, nothing that I have spoken would be unfamiliar to a New Testament scholar, and a scholar of early Christianity. Everything in terms of method that we use we've learned from them . . . .

So, yes, it can be done and should be done wherever the data are available and appropriate, and they are certainly available and appropriate in Judaism and Christianity.

III

CREATING A *BRAHMAN*: A STRUCTURAL APPROACH TO RELIGION

Hans H. Penner

In this paper I am assuming that the study of world religions is similar to the study of anything else in the world. This assumption would be a simple and straightforward statement were it not for the fact that there are many who would disagree with it. There are scholars, for example, who would deny that religion can be studied the same way we study anything else in our world. This position involves a theory and method that is not self-evident, and I have yet to find an adequate explication of the position that does not contradict itself.

There are others who might agree with the statement but find papers and discussions on methodology either tedious or counter-productive. I find this position most perplexing. I can well understand how one can become tired of reflecting upon problems that are theoretical in nature; but when exhaustion becomes a steady state we are indeed at the end of our intellectual journey.

Lack of interest in theoretical issues might indicate that we think we have gone as far as we can go, and all we have to do now is apply what we have. This kind of certainty is very dangerous. In the first place, the history of science shows us that our knowledge of the world is the result of many theories and hypotheses that have been falsified. And, secondly, it is often the case that we become blind to specific problems as a result of our certainty. Thirdly, theoretical certainty often produces forgetfulness. We forget, for example, that it is not only the religions of the world that remain a problem, but also the theories and methods which explain them. We forget that in any science both theory and data are related to each other. And in spite of the talk about the neutrality and normlessness of the study of religion there are assumptions of a metaphysical kind that we are out to prove. For some it may be the point that all religions, and thus all men, are not equal, either rationally or morally. For others, it may be just the reverse: all men are equal, there is a psychic unity to mankind. We can also find a combination of these two assumptions. All men are equal but there is also progress, both cognatively and morally. And, finally, there are authors who think that archaic or primitive man is complete and it is modern man who has degenerated into loss of freedom, reason and morality.

This paper will be a series of reflections on the issues just raised. In other words, it is a reflection on the topic of our symposium: methodology and world religions.

Since understanding and explaining religion is our central concern I will begin with a description of a ritual from Hinduism. Although this ritual comes from a religious tradition with which I am familiar, I am persuaded that we could take data from any religious tradition as our point of departure.

The ritual is called the *upanayana*, and its importance in traditional Hinduism can be described as follows: First, it gives second birth (*dvija*) to a boy. It is the ritual that allows for the study of the Veda which leads to the end of transmigration. Secondly, although we cannot say that the investiture of the sacred thread is the most important ritual, it certainly is highly significant because of the fact that it is a mediating ritual between being a child and being an adult, between being single and being married, between being born and dying. And, thirdly, for those of you who are historically minded, it is a very ancient ritual. We find it recorded in one of the oldest ritual texts of India, the *Shatapatha Brahmana*, and we find it in every collection of major rituals, which are called *Grihya Sutras*. Fourthly, for those of you who are more concerned with contemporary relevance than ancient history, the ritual of drawing near is performed in some form by modern Hindus who wear the sacred thread.[1]

The ritual begins when a boy reaches a certain age. On a day that is carefully selected, the boy begins the day with a last meal with his mother. His religious teacher, the *acarya*, performs certain rituals for himself and the boy in order to purify them both from any offense from previous rituals and actions. The *acarya* then announces that he is ready to perform the ritual so that the boy, becoming twice-born, will be able to know the Vedas.

He takes the boy to the north side of the ritual ground and places him on his right side and wraps a cloth around him three times, while reciting a mantra to Mitravaruna. He then wraps a skin around the boy and repeats a mantra to Ajina. After the skin comes the sacred thread, and the mantra recited is to Paramatma, the supreme self. The mantra is:

> OM, Investiture with the sacred thread is the highest means of purification. It was from the very beginning born together with Prajapati, producing release and radiance. Let the investiture with the sacred thread bring into existence power and brilliance.

Then the boy circles around the fire, walks to the north side and sits down facing west. The teacher faces east. The teacher then performs the supreme oblation to Agni and Prajapati. The boy circles the fire again, ending on the north side, facing west. With water flowing through his hands into the boy's hands, the teacher commits the boy into the protection of Savitri. He announces that the boy has become born, he is a *brahmacarin*, a student and an ascetic. The boy looks up at the sun and the teacher declares that the boy is born. At this point, the boy turns and faces the east. He circles the fire and returns to the north side.

New-born, the teacher ritually invests the boy with the powers of intelligence, sexual potency and bodily vigor, while uttering mantras to Agni. He places ash on the boy's forehead, neck, navel, shoulders and head, and the boy prays for faith, strength, fame, knowledge, wealth and a successful threefold life. Once again, he circles the fire, stops on the north side and faces west.

The boy then pronounces his name and the name of his *gotra*, or family. He states that he desires to learn the Gayatri mantra, which is the most powerful and auspicious mantra of all the Vedas. The teacher recites the mantra and the boy repeats it: "Oh, Savitri, best among the gods, radiant and great, grant us knowledge."

The teacher then places a vow on the heart of the boy by uttering a mantra to Brihaspati, and gives the boy a belt which he ties around his waist with a threefold knot representing the three Vedas. He is also given a staff to protect him from crudeness and lack of self-control. Finally, he is given the rules by which he must live as a student-ascetic.

An oblation is then performed for the assembly and the deity of the oblation is Sadaspati. It ends with the repetition of the great Gayatri mantra to Savitri.

The ritual has now neared its completion. The boy is presented to all the deities and pours out the ritual vessels from the north side of the fire. He gives the teacher his clothes and a fee. The ritual ends with the boy praying to Sadaspati to make him wise, handsome, faithful, trustful and worthy of being heard.

The ritual is, of course, much more complicated than this brief description, but I do think that all of the important features of the ritual are included in this synopsis. The question that immediately comes to mind is, "What is this kind of language and behavior all about? What does it mean?" The first thing that comes to mind is the answer that this is the way Hindus teach their children their religious and moral tradition. Now, this is certainly true. But things become a little more difficult when we ask why Hindu boys learn about their tradition in this kind of way. Why does he have to perform this ritual before he can go on to learn the Vedas? Why is it the case that if he doesn't perform the ritual he will not be able to perform others? Why does he have to go through the rites of purification, have a cloth and a skin wrapped around him, learn a sacred mantra, and circle around a fire, always ending up on the north side facing west? The simplest answer to all these questions is, he does all this because the Hindus have always done it this way. But this simple reply is also an admission that we really don't know why he does what he does.

In looking back over the past few decades with regard to the study of religion there seem to be three ways by which we have attempted to come to grips with rituals such as the one just described. The first approach will be called essentialism, or the phenomenology of religion. The second is usually called functionalism, and the third is known as structuralism. It will be the thesis of this paper that the first two approaches are inadequate and that the third approach, as it develops, may prove to be the right one. Let me point out here that a fourth approach, which might be called the historical approach, has not been included because the other three include it as a part of understanding or explaining religion; that is to say, there is nothing unique about using history in our understanding of religion because all disciplines and methods use history or the traditions of a religion in order to explain particular religious data, such as myths, rituals, philosophies, and the like. It is only when history is turned into a method itself that we might come up with a fourth approach. But this would be similar to saying that history explains history, which sounds rather odd.

Some of you may have noticed that theology has also been excluded. This may seem to be a glaring omission since it is certainly the case that theology (and by theology, I mean Christian theology) has said an awful lot about the religions of the world. In looking over a range of theological possibilities which might be included in this paper I decided to exclude theology for two reasons. First, what many theologians have to say about world religions is based upon a revelation they have received. And, if I understand them correctly, the assertions they make about world religions are not to be taken as theoretical assertions, since revelation is not a theory. In my most adventuresome moments I often think that such expositions should be taken much more seriously by historians of religions because they are part of the religious data we are concerned with.

I am aware of the fact that not all theologians are convinced that revelation is not a theory. And when I read the works of such theologians on myth and religion I am convinced that what they have to say fits into the three approaches I want to discuss. In other words, there is nothing special about their methodology which would deserve the creation of another category alongside the three I have already mentioned. For these reasons, let us concentrate on essentialism, functionalism and structuralism.

The essentialist or phenomenological approach to religion has a long history. I think it is fair to say that its appearance in the study of religion was born out of a reaction against both theological explanations of religion and interpretations of religion which were considered to be "reductive." Its aim has always been to present us with an objective account of religion, and the objectivity of the account had to stand somewhere between dogmatic theology on the one hand, and the "reductive" accounts of the cultural sciences on the other. When phenomenology of religion means more than description or typology we find that this approach to religion contains something worth reflecting upon. This is especially true when we are told that an explanation of religion based upon theology remains dogmatic, while an explanation based upon history, social sentiments, or psychological dispositions remains arbitrary. Dogmatism and arbitrariness are the twin problems that essentialists wish to overcome in the study of religion.

How would a phenomenologist proceed if we gave him the *upanayana* ritual? Since we do not have an actual theory or method to quote from we will have to gather together a set of premises which will describe the starting point rather accurately. First, we must assume that religion is a reality *sui generis*. And, second, we must see that the essence of religion, not its contingent properties, is a sacred or transcendent reality. The drawing near ritual of the Hindu boy is a manifestation of this sacred reality which in itself can only be intuited. The history of religions and the ritual described are appearances of a transcendent, sacred reality.

Given our intuitions concerning the sacred we may then proceed to classify or construct typologies of myths, rituals, religious persons, and other symbols of the sacred. The symbols in the *upanayana* ritual, such as rebirth, the fire in the center, the recitation of mantras, and the various deities (many of whom are creator gods), refer to a sacred reality which all religious traditions imitate in one form or another.

We are told that the greatest strength of a phenomenological approach to religion rests in its objectivity, in its ability to present us with a pure description of religion which is free of norms. Now, if you have read books and articles on religion which have been written from an essentialist point of view it should be obvious that they are not simply descriptions of religious traditions or texts. What do they mean, then, when they speak of a purely objective approach to religion which does not contain any normative judgments? It certainly cannot mean the objectivity of typologies and classifications of religion, since these vary from author to author. The objective description of religion must then refer to the ability to select symbols out of a range of languages and behavior which refer to or manifest the sacred. But how do they do this? There is nothing in the ritual I described which tells us it is an expression of the sacred. Is there something about walking around a fire, or standing north of a fire receiving a belt or a staff that would lead us to conclude that this behavior expresses a transcendent, *sui generis* reality? Is there something awesome, dreadful or fascinating about the ritual? Perhaps it is the bizarreness of the whole event that leads us to the sacred. But, then we must ask, bizarre for whom, the phenomenologist or the Hindu?

The problem with the essentialist ability to select certain symbols as expressions of the sacred is based upon the fact that from a phenomenological point of view the term "sacred" is not a theoretical term but an essence which can only be intuited. Thus, our ability to determine which symbols, among a variety of expressions, are sacred symbols is dependent upon either our own intuition or the acceptance of the intuition of others.

Phenomenologists tell us that they do not make any normative judgments concerning which of the symbols has greater value as a disclosure of the sacred. In fact, we are sometimes told that the symbols are all of equal value. It is not necessary for our purposes to check and see whether phenomenologists have consistently maintained that all religious symbols are of equal value. We have learned from them that religion is both fascinating and dreadful, awesome and awful, and that the manifestations of the sacred take on a variety of forms.

What the essentialist fails to notice is that his descriptions or typologies of religious symbols are not the stumbling block of his approach. The fundamental problem is the assertion that rituals such as the *upanayana* are manifestations of the sacred, and that this transcendent reality cannot be known. The consequences of such assertions can only lead us back to the problems which phenomenology seeks to overcome.

Let us simply assume for the moment that we are all capable of intuiting the essence of religion as a transcendent reality. Let us also assume that it makes sense to say that the essence of religion is a reality that is *sui generis*, a reality wholly other. I can only conclude that the consequences of such premises will lead us to a position in which we must admit that our descriptions and typologies refer to something that cannot be known, but only intuited. And since we cannot construct a theory about the essence of religion without entering into a normative discussion about our intuitions, we are left with assertions about religion that are neither true nor false.

The fact that we can check the historical, linguistic, and textual accuracy of what a phenomenologist has to say about religion is irrelevant at this point. Such tests are not unique to phenomenology. What we need in order to check the objectivity of an essentialist's account of religion is a way of testing the assertion that the reference of religious symbols, the essence of religion, is a transcendent reality, which in itself can only be intuited. Since this cannot be done we are left with the conclusion that the reference of religious symbolism is a mystery, which is another way of saying that the history of religions itself will remain an inexplicable mystery. But a science of religion based upon a mystery remains a mysterious science. We are left with either accepting phenomenological typologies and classifications as arbitrary, thus contradicting the claim of objectivity, or believing in the intuitions of individual scholars concerning the sacred, which lands us in dogmatism. In either case, the development of a science of religion remains impossible.

Our second approach, which is known as functionalism, is by far the most popular approach to religion. It is persuasive because it is rooted in the conviction that the study of religion must be logically rigorous and empirically verifiable. According to functional theory we simply will not be able to explain the *upanayana* ritual by speculating on its origins, intuiting its essence, or by placing it on some evolutionary schema. What we need to do is to stop trying to intuit essences, get out of our armchairs and into the field where religion really exists.

Now, it would appear that essentialism and functionalism are radical alternatives to the study of religion. In a way this is certainly true. But phenomenologists often borrow the notion of function as a way which satisfies our need or thirst for the sacred. The difference between the two at this point has to do with the referent of the symbols. Essentialists often say that functionalists are "reductionists" when they assert that the only function of religion is the satisfaction of social or psychological needs.[2] And functionalists often call essentialists mystics or theologians because of their emphasis on the intuition of a transcendent reality. But on the whole, things have gone rather well. From an essentialist point of view, what functionalists have to say about religion is true as long as we remember that the essence of religion belongs to phenomenology.

Although it is true that not all functionalists are capable of stating their theory without confusion, the premises of contemporary functionalism have been worked out rather clearly. The stress is on the point that functional explanations of religion are causal explanations of a particular kind. A functional explanation of the ritual described at the beginning of this paper will seek to explain it by reference to its consequences for a social system. This means that functionalism will not be able to explain *why* the *upanayana* ritual, or the use of mantras, or polytheism appeared in Hinduism and not, for example, in Islam. An explanation of this kind would explain the ritual by reference to antecedent conditions together with relevant laws. A good functional argument will admit that our knowledge of the antecedent conditions of the *upanayana* ritual is arbitrary and that we simply do not have anything that would come close to meeting the requirements of a law of history or culture.

We may begin a functional explanation with what appears to be an empirical statement that society in India functions adequately. It does so because certain needs which are necessary to its existence are being satisfied. It is an empirical fact that Hinduism is a religious institution within a social system, and the *upanayana* ritual is a particular unit in the religious institution. We can explain the ritual if we can show that it functions to satisfy certain necessary needs of Indian society.

It took someone sitting in a reflective armchair to shake many of us out of our contentment with this theory. I don't think Carl Hempel has ever been out in the field, nor has he tried to intuit the essence of religion. Simply interested in the logic of functional explanations, he took a look at them and made it clear from his analysis that such explanations are false, trivial or tautologous.

Since his analysis is sometimes overlooked or misunderstood I want to repeat it with some comments of my own. It is an excellent illustration of why we should concern ourselves with theories and methods in the study of religion, for it shows that criticism of a widespread theory of religion is just as important for the development of our knowledge as are the bold hypotheses which lead us to new discoveries.

Hempel's first example of a functional explanation is presented in the following way:

1. At *t*, *S* functions adequately in a setting of kind *c* (characterized by specific internal and external conditions).

2. *S* functions adequately in a setting of kind *c* only if a certain necessary condition *n* is satisfied.

3. If trait *i* were present in *S*, then, as an effect condition *n* would be satisfied.

4. (Hence) at *t*, trait *i* is present in *S*.[3]

There are three important points I want to make with regard to this example. First, Hempel states that the society functions adequately "only if a certain necessary condition is satisfied." I believe every functionalist would agree with this premise. It is the rule which asserts that some condition is necessary for the maintenance of a society. Secondly, the example is an accurate representation of functional explanations in that the third premise states, "if trait *i* were present in *S*, then, as an effect condition *n* would be satisfied." In other words, premise three is a way of stating the point stressed by all contemporary functionalists, that we explain religion, for example, by reference to its consequences, that is, by the effect it has on the system. Thirdly, the conclusion is false. All we can conclude is that "somehow" the needs of a society are being satisfied; but this is not only trivial, it is not what we started out to explain. What we want is an explanation that will causally explain the *upanayana* ritual as a function of need satisfaction. The fallacy can be corrected so that the explanation does not commit us to either a logical blunder or triviality.

The correction gives us the second example:

1. At *t*, *S* functions adequately in a setting of kind *c* (characterized by specific internal and external conditions).

2. *S* functions adequately in a setting of kind *c* only if a certain necessary condition *n* is satisfied.

3. *Only if* trait *i* were present, then as an effect condition *n* would be satisfied.

4.   (Hence) at t, trait i is present in S.

This revision of the explanation now states that the particular religious trait we are out to explain is a necessary trait for the existence of a society. I know of no functionalist who would want to maintain that a religious trait, or any other social trait, is a necessary condition for the existence of a society, and the notion of functional equivalents, or functional substitutes, is sound evidence from within functionalism to show that the assertion of a "necessary trait" cannot be sustained.

Given this problem, we move to a third model of functional explanation. The first premise remains the same:

1.   At t, S functions adequately in a setting of kind c (characterized by specific internal and external conditions).

The second premise also remains unchanged:

2. S functions adequately in a setting of kind c only if a certain necessary condition n is satisfied.

The third premise is revised. It now reads:

3. I is the class of empirically sufficient conditions for n, in the context determined by S and c; and I is not empty.

From these premises we can conclude that:

4.   Some one of the items included in I is present in S at t.

The explanation is certainly valid, but the point is that the conclusion once again is trivial. All we can conclude is that "somehow" the society is functioning adequately.

The rejoinder might be raised here that these examples are really irrelevant. Functionalism is much more complicated than this since the causal explanation involves the use of a feedback system. If this is true, it means that an explanation of a religious trait or property in a feedback system must meet the following conditions. First, we must be able to assert what property is being maintained in a steady state. Second, we must be able to describe the internal variables of the system and measure their effects or consequences. And third, we must be able to state the external conditions which are assumed to be constant.[4]

It is obvious that it will be exceedingly difficult to meet the requirements of a feedback model in order to explain the function of religion. In fact, I know of no functional explanation which has come close to meeting any of them. But let us assume that some day it will be possible to meet the requirements of explaining religion as a trait or unit in a feedback system. When this happens it will also entail the assertion that religion is a necessary trait in the system. In other words, we are back to Hempel's second model of a functional explanation and the problems it raises.

Most contemporary functionalists are aware of the problems I have raised. If we read their explanations carefully what we find is the more cautious statement that religion "tends" to satisfy a certain condition, or "may" satisfy a social need, or that religion is among a "range of alternatives" that singly or together function to satisfy the necessary conditions of a society. But such explanations are far from satisfactory because they entail our third model of a functional explanation. Furthermore, tendency statements are neither true nor false for they cannot be tested.

Our reflections on the essentialist and functionalist approaches to religion lead us to the same conclusion. It is not the problem that one of them is metaphysical and the other is reductionist. The conclusion we must come to is that the assertions which are made in both essentialism and functionalism cannot be verified. This means that the history of religions remains inexplicable, if not incomprehensible.

The task of constructing an approach to religion which will avoid the problems uncovered in both phenomenology and functionalism is not an easy one. However, the weaknesses in both approaches contain something positive; they show us what we need to avoid. I think that the contemporary development of structuralism may lead us in the right direction. The theory and method are best known to us from the discipline of linguistics, but the approach is also used in anthropology, psychology, biology and mathematics. It is a theory that will hopefully overcome the splintering effect of autonomous disciplines in a multiversity.

I think R.G. Runciman is quite right in pointing out that the term "structure" means system.[5] But care must be taken so that structural approaches to religion are differentiated from others which use the same term in a different way. I want to point out the main premises so that we have them clearly in mind as we proceed.

First, it is important to remember that structuralism is formal and rational. By this, I mean that the theory seeks to provide us with rules for the analysis of religion that are not dependent upon psychological dispositions, social sentiments, or the contingencies of history. This clearly distinguishes the contemporary use of structure from its older use as it is found in the works of such scholars as Radcliffe-Brown and Durkheim. For although Durkheim and Radcliffe-Brown saw the significance of society as a system of rules, they based this system on certain dispositions or sentiments and then went on to identify the system with empirically identifiable traits or units which were found in the society.

One of the central premises in structuralism is the denial that structure is identical with observable relations of social units or traits. Such observations are the "surface structure," if I can use that phrase, and although the surface structure is necessary for formal analysis it will not of itself give us the "deep structure" which constitutes the system. The notion of system must be distinguished from empirically observable traits, or units. The deep structure is a theoretical postulate which can be verified by the observations we have at our disposal.

One of the implications of all this is that it is rather useless to go around asking persons of a certain religious tradition for the structure or system of their religion. Our task is to construct the formal model which in turn will explain the empirical facts of a religion. In its most successful stage, structural analysis is formal analysis.

These basic starting points should elicit much greater controversy from historians of religion than they have in the past, for they clearly argue against the essentialism of phenomenology, the empiricism of functionalism, and the arbitrariness of historical approaches which operate on the thesis that we can uncover the structure or system of a religion by tracing its history. It should also be obvious that the term structure as I have just described it is not identical with its vague use in typologies, patterns and classifications of religion.

A structural approach to religion will emphasize the wholeness of the system, and the transformational rules which constitute the basis for the self-regulation of the religious system in both its continuity and change.

The study of the origin of structures which is being made in other disciplines should also allow us to open up the question of the origin of religious structures once again. We should be able to work out an answer to this question which will clearly avoid the perplexing alternatives of either founding the origin of religious structures in eternal essences or innateness on the one hand, or the arbitrariness of contingent emergence on the other.

With these remarks as a preface, I want to submit the following premises as minimum hypotheses which may help us out of some of our dilemmas in the study of religion. First, the study of religion is an aspect of the study of man, and this means that we have no need for unique theories, methods or intuitions. Second, religion is a group institution, a system, and the rules of this system are imposed upon individuals. Third, the language of religion, both verbal and nonverbal, remains independent of the decisions of individuals. Fourth, the individual members of a religion are often unaware of the structural model which constitutes their religion. This means that it is quite misleading to emphasize the history of a religion in order to explain it or to ask an individual for the structure of his religion.

Given these premises as a minimum hypothesis for the study of religion we can return to the ritual that was described and make the following remarks about it. First of all, we may note what Van Gennep discovered long ago: the ritual is a rite of passage. We can define the structure of the ritual as a mediation between a pre-liminal stage and a post-liminal stage. The boy begins the ritual with a meal with his mother. He will leave the ritual as an ascetic, a student, who will beg for his meals. He begins the ritual dependent upon his mother; he will leave the ritual dependent upon his religious teacher. In other words, the liminal stage *is* the ritual; it can be seen as the mediation which provides for a transformation from boy to ascetic, or student. It is precisely this liminality which has proved to be so perplexing to students of religion.

Let us now turn to the structure of the ritual. Besides the cloth, thread, staff and belt that are given the boy, you may have noticed the repeated emphasis on circling the fire, standing to the north of it and facing west. This ritual prescription becomes intelligible when we remember that from the time of the Brahmanas, that is, from pre-Buddhist times, Hinduism has not only placed great significance upon the four directions of space, north-south, east-west, but has also ordered gods, demons, ancestors and man according to the four directions. Thus, the north is also equivalent to man and the dawn; the east is equivalent to gods and daytime, the south to ancestors and twilight, and the west to the demons and night.

A simple diagram may help illustrate this structure as it is found in both myth and ritual in Hinduism. (See Figure 1.)

The ritual can be seen as a series of mediations or transformations of opposite pairs. We not only have the pairs of north/south and east/west, but also gods/demons, man/ancestor, creation/destruction and life/death. These pairs are mediated by the positions of the boy and the religious teacher who, while standing north of the fire, face west and east respectively. Thus, north mediates between east and west, as man mediates between gods and demons, as life mediates between creation and destruction. And, if we take the directions which the boy and the religious teacher face we find that in this liminal stage in

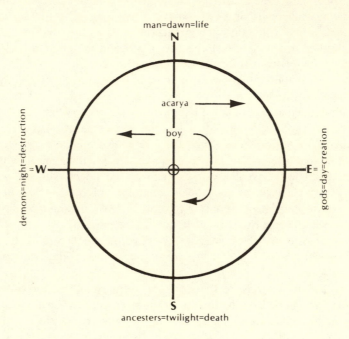

FIGURE 1

the life of a Hindu, the boy is to demons as the religious teacher
is to gods.

Now, I find it quite significant that at the very point where a
brahman is created in this ritual, the point, that is to say, where the
Hindu boy becomes twice-born, we find the directions reversed. After
the boy has put on the cloth, skin and thread, and after he has walked
around the fire several times, always ending up on the north side of the
fire facing west, the religious teacher announces "OM. This youth
wearing the splendid clothes around him becomes born." Immediately
after this the boy reverses directions and faces the east. This gives us
the following pairs: north/east, man/gods, south/west, ancestors/demons
or life/creation and death/destruction. It is after this point in the ritual
that the boy recites his name and receives the Gayatri mantra. Then he
circles the fire once more, only to reverse his position again by

facing west, which is the way the ritual begins, but now the boy is an ascetic rather than a son.

The structure of the ritual for creating a *brahman* can be described as follows. The first thing we noticed was that the ritual involves a series of pairs. The ritual diagram and the *upanayana* itself allows us to rewrite these pairs into a series of mediations: north mediates east/west as man mediates gods/demons as life mediates creation/destruction.

We have now reached the point where we can explain how a boy becomes an ascetic (or student), *how* the structure of the ritual constitutes a rite of passage. The orientation of the ritual, north of the fire, indicates it is a ritual for man, for becoming born a second time. Taking into consideration the directions which the boy and the teacher face we may rewrite the mediations as follows: man (boy) is to demons and destruction as man (religious teacher) is to gods and creation. By reversing the directions we find: man (boy) is to gods and creation as life is to creation and destruction, which is where the ritual began. Only now it will be the boy who pours out the ritual vessels from the north of the fire and not the religious teacher, as at the beginning of the ritual.

Finally, in looking at the deities of the mantras we notice the following list: Prajapati, Rudra, Savitri, Varuna, Sadaspati, Agni and Brihaspati. Once we know who they are we find the following pairs once again: Creator/destroyer, light/darkness, dwelling place/fire, and, finally, Brihaspati who is literally a "mediator," one who intercedes.

This brief and not very elegant analysis shows us that ritual is more than just the sum of its units. It is a system of communication based upon rules of transformation which allow for both continuity and change. It contains the syntax which allows a Hindu to pass from boy to ascetic. Although my analysis may be rather crude, I think it can be formalized. I submit the further hypothesis that if we place the *upanayana* back into the series of rituals which precede and succeed it (rituals of birth and marriage, for example), we will find the same system.

I also think that this kind of approach may lead us to new insights with regard to texts and rituals on classical Yoga and the Sankhya system. If most of the rituals we are familiar with involve a structure which is the basis for a change, or passage from boy to *brahman*, from being single to being married, the ritual structure of Yoga may be analyzed as constant liminality, or liminal stasis. The Sankhya system with its remarkable emphasis on oppositions would represent the verbal counterpart to the non-verbal behavior in the Yoga system. Yoga, from this point of view, is not a rite *for* passage but a *rite of stasis,* holding the liminal constant. We know the consequences of such stress on the liminal; it is silence.

I am sure there are many problems in my analysis. One of the most serious problems is the problem of meaning. Is the structure of the ritual its meaning? Can we integrate form and content? I want to say yes, but realize that this is one of the most difficult questions we face. From the analysis presented in this paper we can already see the inadequacies of answers which state that the meaning of religion is the sacred of a symbolic representation of social relations. In my second paper I shall try to uncover why this is the case.

DISCUSSION

Baird—The question that you raised about functionalism was that it would not be able to explain why the *upanayana* ritual or the use of mantras, or polytheism, appeared in Hinduism and not, for example, in Islam.

The crucial word here is "why."

Now when you get finished spelling out the possible contribution of structure and structuralism, you indicate we've now reached the point where we can explain *how* a boy becomes an ascetic or a student, *how* the structure of the ritual constitutes a rite of passage; in other words, I would be quite willing to admit that you have explained *how* it takes place, but I wonder if in fact you have done any better than the functionalists in explaining *why* it has taken place here rather than elsewhere.

Penner—I would say two things about it:

I have not *causally* explained it in a functional sense, so I am not able to talk about its consequences, and so forth. Or in a society, for obviously, in the kind of structuralism I tried to work out, this is a different kind of explication of the principles.

. . . I can't really say *why* it is the case, because . . . the "why" element would have to be formalized. I would have to give you the postulates in the "deep structure" of that crude model that I gave you that generates that system . . . . I have not been able to do that. That would be the difference.

My question here is no longer the explanation of something by its consequence to the needs of a society. There would be the difference.

Question—When you talk about structure, you are saying . . . with reference to the rite, that the elements of the rite are analogous to the phonemes and the syntax of language?

Penner—No, I don't want to say that . . . .

Question—Isn't what you see as a positive element in structuralism, that it can get, as the science of linguistics does, to the basic syntax, the basic phoneme, things which people are not conscious of, and if you're not willing to make that analogy, then I ask where does the force of your argument of structuralism go?

Penner—. . . I think that linguist structuralists are now on their way to give us also the semantic component in the structure. Until 1965, that wasn't even mentioned.

Question—If semantics will remain a mystery, then why does not the *upanayana* too?

Penner—I don't think it will.

I think the semantic components, the syntactic and the semantic components, both are necessary conditions for any linguistic theory.

Question—If we grant for the moment that you correctly "unpacked" the *upanayana* ritual as a mediation of these binary opposites . . . . I'm still uncertain as to where the binary opposites come from. To what does one appeal? Is there some sort of existential anxiety in the members of the tradition that gives them a sense of tension? What is the origin of the binary opposites?

Penner—I would say, the member of the tradition perceives whatever tensions he has in life because of the structure, because of the constitution, because of the structure and how that constitutes his language, his capacity for communication, etc., in both continuity and change in this particular religious tradition.

The meaning, the syntax and semantics of it, has to be seen and explicated in terms of the structure.

Question—Are you suggesting that the actual structure comes before the experience of life?

Penner—I am given the language before I am able to speak it. That's the analogy I'm following. Language is given to me. I have no choice in that . . . .

Question—Are you then willing to say you don't know yet where these "deep structures" are, in an ontological sense, i.e., [are they] in the mind, in the genes, in the Jungian collective unconscious?

Penner—It's a constructionist vs. innateness kind of thing. I think innateness is not an answer, and many people have criticized Chomsky for that, but I would go so far as to maintain that at this point at least it is a theoretical postulate that I think people can continue to look at, and we will know at some point or another whether it is true or false. Now if it's false, we've learned a lot . . . .

Question—Do you think it makes any difference for the study of religion if "deep structures" describe a certain intra-mental process or describe a certain process of relationships between men?

Penner—I think there will be a big difference here, because if we're not careful we're going to say that theoretical postulates and theoretical constructions [are] essentialism.

But I think *empirically* it is the case, just as in astrophysics, we can postulate certain things and verify them in terms of the isomorphic relationship between what we have constructed and what is the world.

But this again is not essentialism. There's no doubt that there's something metaphysical under this: that there's a psychic unity to mankind.

What I would like is a theoretical postulate where I could show it *is* the case that this is true. Heretofore we've not been able to do this.

Question—Can a structuralist account for changes in the system? Can you have new "deep structures"?

Penner—Our problem is the *history* of religions. As long as we go after the accumulation of a tradition we're never going to make it. History's going to change.

Question—You were suggesting that in certain ways the historical method, generally construed, underlies each of your three alternatives. Does it underlie the third alternative as you sketched it out and if so, how?

Were you appealing to the history of Indian religion in the notion of the four directions or were you appealing to structuralism, and what is the nexus between the two?

Penner—. . . The analytic, the intensional, precedes the extension. The formal, the analytic, the given, must precede the surface of what I want to explicate, or otherwise I can't explicate it. That is the nexus between the two . . . .

IV

THE STUDY OF TRADITION
AS RELIGION IN JUDAISM

Jacob Neusner

For nearly 20 centuries the central and predominant commitment of Rabbinic Judaism, that is, that form of Judaism deemed normative and generative of the Judaic understanding of existence, has been to learning, and specifically, to what is called "study of Torah." "Study of Torah" is understood in a very specific way, as devotion to the learning both of the Scriptures, held to be the written revelation of God to Moses at Sinai, and of the *Torah shebe al peh*, the Oral revelation, concomitant with the written one. "The whole Torah of Moses"—oral or written—constituted the sum and substance of Rabbinic Judaism, its claim upon legitimacy and spiritual hegemony in Israel. The history of Judaism, therefore, is primarily the work of men who believed that at the center of the religious life lies the act of learning, at the focus of the experience of the sacred is the activity of the mind.

In the literature of Rabbinic Judaism we find numerous sayings to express this most fundamental conviction, for instance, "Piety without learning in Torah is impossible." "Study of Torah outweighs all else." It goes without saying that Rabbinism furthermore maintained everyone is to become learned and, in its healthiest moments, made provision for all classes of male Israelites to join the Rabbinic estate, to study and master Torah. My purpose is to analyze this mode of religious expression and to explain what is, or can be, religious about learning.

Let me first distinguish Rabbinic intellectualism from Western scholarship. To the rabbi, the question of Tertullian, "What has Athens to do with Jerusalem, the Academy with the Church?" has no meaning. He could not have grasped a distinction between the piety of the synagogue and the activity of the academy, the *yeshivah*. The one was the pale reflection of the other. Since, as I shall stress, God is not only revealer of the Torah, but also studies Torah in a heavenly academy, what man does below is a reflection of the true reality above. To ask what learning has to do with piety, one to begin with would have to conceive of God as other than master of Torah and the imitation of God as other than learning. Such a conception lies wholly outside the Rabbinic framework. The rabbi likewise cannot grasp the question, "What is the use of it all?" For to him, the answer is too obvious to legitimate the question. Perceiving no distinction between intellect and soul or spirit, he cannot wonder about the relationship between learning and devotion, between mind and spirit. If he is a mystic, and many have been, he composes a book on mystical doctrine, not merely experiencing mystical reality. If he is a philosopher, his philosophy becomes a mode of Torah. If he is a lawyer, the mastery of the law is the highest expression of his piety; the study of details of the law is holy in itself.

Clearly, this total integration of faith and intellect, both at its most fundamental level and in its most superficial effects, is the result of the apprehension of a profoundly mythic conception of life, of the perfect correspondence between myth and reality interpreted by myth. Let me therefore turn to the Torah-myth of Rabbinic Judaism and explain its substance. The encompassing myth revealed by Rabbinic Judaism centers upon the figure of Moses and tells the story of the Moses-piety—spirituality centered on Moses—of the rabbis. That story relates God's disclosure to Moses of a dual revelation, or Torah, at Mount Sinai, one in writing, the other handed orally from master to disciple. The whole Torah, oral and written, contains the design for the universe, the divine architect's plan for reality. It is to be studied, therefore, not merely for information, but as an act of piety and reverence for the divine lawgiver. Just as God teaches Torah to Moses, so the rabbi, modeling his life after Moses "our rabbi," teaches his own disciple. In "studying Torah," and even more so in effecting it in the lives of Israel, the rabbi thus imitates God. Following the model of the "school" in heaven, the schools for Torah-study bring together masters and disciples and preserve the ancient traditions.

The most striking aspect of these schools is the rabbis' conception that in them live holy men, men who more accurately than anyone else conform to the image of God conveyed by divine revelation through the Torah of Moses "our rabbi." The schools are not holy places only or primarily in the sense that pious people make pilgrimages to them or that miracles are supposed to take place there. The schools are holy because there men achieve sainthood through study of Torah and imitation of the conduct of the masters. In doing so, they conform to the heavenly paradigm, the Torah, believed to have been created by God "in his image," revealed at Sinai, and handed down to their own teachers. Thus obedience to the teachings of the rabbis leads not merely to ethical or moral goodness, but to holiness or sainthood. Discussion of legal traditions, rather than ascetic disciplines or long periods of fasting and prayer, is the rabbis' way to holiness.

If the masters and disciples obey the divine teaching of Moses our rabbi, then their society, the school, replicates on earth the heavenly academy, just as the disciple incarnates the heavenly model of Moses our rabbi. The rabbis believe that Moses is a rabbi, God dons phylacteries, and the heavenly court studies Torah precisely as does the earthly one, even arguing about the same questions. These beliefs today may be seen as projections of rabbinical values onto heaven, but the rabbis believe that they themselves are projections of heavenly values onto earth. The rabbis thus conceive that on earth they study Torah just as God, the angels, and Moses our rabbi do in heaven. The heavenly schoolmen are even aware of scholastic discussions, so they require a rabbi's information about an aspect of purity-taboos.

So the rabbis believe that the man truly made in the divine image is the rabbi; he embodies revelation, both oral and written, and all his actions constitute paradigms that are not merely correct, but holy and heavenly. Rabbis enjoy exceptional grace from heaven. Torah is held to be a source of supernatural power. The rabbis control the power of Torah because of their mastery of its contents. They furthermore use their own mastery of Torah quite independent of heavenly action. They issue blessings and curses, create men and animals, and master witchcraft, incantations, and amulets. They communicate with heaven. Their Torah is sufficiently effective to thwart the action of demons. However much they disapprove of other people's magic, they themselves do the things magicians do.

The rabbis furthermore want to transform the entire Jewish community into an academy where the whole Torah was studied and kept. This belief aids in understanding the rabbis' view that Israel will be redeemed through Torah. Because Israel had sinned, it was punished by being given over into the hands of earthly empires; when it atones, it will be removed from their power. The means of this atonement or reconciliation are study of Torah, practice of commandments, and doing good deeds. These transform each Jew into a rabbi, hence into a saint. When all Jews become rabbis, they then will no longer lie within the power of history. The Messiah will come. So redemption depends upon the "rabbinization" of all Israel, that is, upon the attainment by all Jewry of a full and complete embodiment of revelation or Torah, thus achieving a perfect replica of heaven. When Israel on earth becomes such a replica, it will be able, as a righteous and saintly community, to exercise the supernatural power of Torah, just as some rabbis are already doing. With access to the consequent theurgical capacities, redemption will naturally follow. The issues of Rabbinic analysis, while rationally investigated, thus are transcendent and cosmic in significance.

If in other religious traditions holiness is expressed through ascetic, flesh-suppressing disciplines, through sitting on pillars or dwelling in caves, through eating only wormwood and dressing only in rags, the rabbis' sainthood consists in the analysis of trivial and commonplace things through practical and penetrating logic and criticism. Their chief rite is *argument*. To be sure, they pray like other people, but to them, learning in Torah is peculiarly "ours," praying is "theirs"—that of ordinary folk. Their heroes are men of learning, and they turned their biblical heroes, beginning with Moses, into men of learning.

The rabbis conceive of practical and critical thinking as holy, claim sainthood in behalf of learned men, see as religiously significant, indeed as sanctified, what the modern intellectual perceives as the very instrument of secularity: the capacity to think critically and to reason. Here is the mystery of Rabbinic Judaism: the (to us) alien and remote conviction that the intellect is an instrument not of unbelief and desacralization but of sanctification. That conviction is the most difficult aspect of Rabbinism to comprehend, because it is so easy to misunderstand and misrepresent. The external form of the belief, our ability to think clearly, to be mindful, is readily accessible to us. But the meaning of the belief, its substance, its place in the shaping of the religious imagination and the formation of the religious and traditional culture of the Jewish people—these are not so obvious.

To grasp the meaning of Rabbinic intellectualism, therefore, we have to turn to its substance, its conception of the world, man, and God. The presupposition of the Rabbinic apporach to life is that order is better than chaos, reflection than whim, decision than accident, ratio-cination and rationality than witlessness and force. The only admissible force is the power of fine logic, ever refined against the gross matter of daily living. The sole purpose is so to construct the discipline of everyday life and to pattern the relationships among men that all things are intelligible, well-regulated, trustworthy—and sanctified. Rabbinic Juda-ism stands for the perfect intellectualization of life, that is, the subjection of life to rational study. For nothing is so trivial as to be unrelated to some conceptual, abstract principle. If the placing of a napkin or the washing of the hands is subject to critical analysis, what can be remote from rigorous inquiry? But the mode of inquiry is not man's alone. Man is made in God's image. And that part of man which is like God is not corporeal. It is the thing which separates man from beast: the mind, consciousness. When man uses his mind, he is acting like God. That surely is a conviction uncharacteristic of modern intellectuals, yet at the heart of Rabbinic intellectuality.

Rabbinic Judaism single-mindedly pursues unifying truths. But that search does not derive from the perception of unifying order in the natural world. It comes, rather, from the lessons imparted supernaturally in the Torah. The sages perceive the Torah not as a mélange of sources and laws of different origins, but as a single, unitary document, a corpus of laws reflective of an underlying ordered will. The Torah reveals the way things should be, just as the rabbis' formulation and presentation of their laws tell how things should be, whether or not that is how they actually are done. The order derives from the plan and will of the Creator of the world, the foundation of all reality. The Torah is inter-preted by the rabbis to be the architect's design for reality: God looked into the Torah and created the world, just as an architect follows his prior design in raising a building. A single, whole Torah—in two forms, oral and written, to be sure—underlies the one, seamless reality of the world. The search for the unities hidden by the pluralities of the trivial world, the supposition that some one thing is revealed by many things: these represent in intellectual form the theological and metaphysical conception of a single, unique God, creator of heaven and earth, revealer of one complete Torah, guarantor of the unity and ultimate meaning of all the human actions and events that constitute history. On that account Rabbinism links the private deeds of man to a larger pattern, provides a large and general "meaning" for small, particular, trivial doings.

Behind this conception of the unifying role of reason and of law and the integrating force of practical criticism of everyday behavior lies the conviction that God supplies the model for man's mind; therefore man, through reasoning in the Torah's laws, may penetrate into God's intent and plan. The rabbis believe they study Torah as God does in heaven; their schools are conducted like the academy on high. They perform rites just as God performed rites, wearing fringes as He does, putting on phylacteries just as God put on phylacteries. In studying Torah, they seek to conform to the heavenly paradigm, revealed by God "in his image" and handed down from Moses and the prophets to their own teachers. If the rabbis study and realize the divine teaching of Moses, whom they call "our rabbi," it is because the order they impose upon earthly affairs replicates on earth the order they perceive from heaven, the rational construction of reality. It is Torah which reveals the mind of God, the principles by which he shapes reality. So studying Torah is not merely imitating God, who does the same, but is a way to apprehension of God and the attainment of the sacred. The modes of argument are holy because they lead from earth to heaven, as prayer or fasting or self-denial cannot. Reason is God's way, and the holy man is therefore he who is able to think clearly and penetrate profoundly into the mysteries of the Torah and, especially, of its so very trivial laws. In context, those trivialities contain revelation.

What is distinctively Rabbinic is perpetual skepticism, expressed in response to every declarative sentence or affirmative statement. Once one states that matters are so, it is inevitable that he will find as a response: "Why do you think so?" Or, "Perhaps things are the opposite of what you say?" Or, "How can you say so when a contrary principle may be adduced?" Articulation, forthrightness, subtle reasoning but lucid expression, skepticism: these are the traits of intellectuals, not of untrained and undeveloped minds, nor of scholars, capable only to serve as curators of the past, but not as critics of the present.

Above all, Rabbinic thinking rejects gullibility and credulity. It is, indeed, peculiarly modern in its systematic skepticism, its testing of each proposition, not to destroy but to refine what people suppose to be so. The Talmud's first question is not "Who says so?" but, "Why?" "What is the reason of the House of Shammai?" In the Rabbinic approach to thought, faith is restricted to ultimate matters, to the fundamental principles of reality beyond which one may not penetrate.

Let us dwell on the centrality of skepticism in the Rabbinic mode of thinking. Virtually as soon as the primary document of the Oral Torah, the Mishnah, or law-code of Judah the Patriarch, reached its present form at the beginning of the 3rd century A.D., the process of criticism and skeptical inquiry began. The people who received the oral tradition, the *Amoraim*, engaged in a far-reaching search for imperfections in the Mishnah, in the certainty of its ultimate perfection. It must have taken considerable courage to criticize an authoritative law-code, the Mishnah, and its accompanying supplement, the Tosefta. It would have been pious merely to accept those laws and digest them for future generations to memorize and copy. Judah the Patriarch, called "our holy rabbi," and those whose traditions he organized and handed on were very ancient authorities. Two or three centuries later, the prestige of the Mishnah, regarded, as we saw, as the "Oral Torah" revealed by Moses at Sinai, was considerable. To ask for reasons, to criticize those reasons, to seek contradictions, to add to the law, to revise or even reject what the ancients had said—these are acts of men who have or lay no equivalent claim either to firsthand knowledge of the Oral Torah or to the sanctity and prestige of the *Tannaim*. Yet that is exactly what the *Amoraim* did. And they did so in such a way as to revise everything that had gone before, to place upon the whole heritage of the past the indelible and distinct, unmistakeable stamp of their own minds.

The reason is that the *Amoraim* did not confuse respect with servility. They carefully nurtured the disciples' critical and creative faculties. Gibbon said (probably unfairly) of the Byzantine schools, "Not a single composition of history, philosophy, or literature has been saved from oblivion by the intrinsic beauties of style, or sentiment, or original fancy, or even of successful imitation." By contrast, the Talmud and later Rabbinic writings are the product not of servility to the past or of dogmatism in the present, but of an exceptionally critical, autonomous rationalism and an utterly independent spirit. The *Amoraim* and later authorities gave to pedantry a cool welcome. Clearly, to them mere learning is insufficient. Not what one knows, but what he can do with what he knows, is decisive. The authority and approbation of the elders are set aside by the critical accomplishments of the newest generation. In the fullest sense, the *Amoraim* and their heirs are not traditionalists. They take the laws and traditions of the early generations into their care, respectfully learning them, reverently handing them on. But these they thoroughly digest and make their own. Their minds are filled with the learning of the ancients. But the irrational wisdom and unrelenting criticism are wholly their own.

The Rabbinic stress upon criticism produces a new freedom of construction, the freedom to reinterpret reality and to reconstruct its artifacts upon the basis of well-analyzed, thoroughly criticized principles revealed through the practical reason of the sages. Once a person is free to stand apart from what is customary and habitual, to restrain energies and regulate them, he attains the higher freedom to revise the given, to reinterpret established perceptions of reality and the institutions which give them effect. This constitutes, to begin with, the process of the mind's focusing upon unseen relationships and the formation of imposed, non-material and non-natural considerations. We recall in this connection the purity laws, which play so considerable a role in the rabbis' regulation of eating (and other fundamental things, for instance, sexual relations). Those laws seem to have comprised and created a wholly abstract set of relationships, a kind of non-Euclidean geometry of the levitical realm. Yet those high abstractions are brought down to earth to determine in what order one washes his hands and picks up a cup of wine or where one puts his napkin. So what is wholly relative and entirely a matter of theory, not attached to concrete things, transforms trivialities. It affects, indeed generates, the way one does them. It transforms them to the higher meanings (to be sure, without much rational, let alone material substance) associated with the pure and the impure. The purity laws stand at the pinnacle of Rabbinic abstraction and ratiocination.

Rabbinic criticism is in four modes: (1) abstract, rational criticism of each tradition in sequence and of the answers hazarded to the several questions; (2) historical criticism of sources and their (un)harmonious relationship; (3) philological and literary criticism of the meanings of words and phrases; and (4) practical criticism of what people actually do in order to carry out their religious obligations. It goes without saying that these four modes of criticism are peculiarly contemporary. Careful, skeptical examination of answers posed to problems is utterly commonplace to modern men and women. Historical criticism of sources, which does not gullibly accept whatever is alleged as fact, is the beginning of historical study. Philological study of the origins and meanings of words, literary criticism of the style of expression—these are familiar. Finally, we take for granted that it is normal to examine peoples' actions against some large principle of behavior. These are traits of inquiry which are both Talmudic and routinely modern.

What makes them different from modern modes of thought? It is the remarkable claim that in the give and take of argument, in the processes of criticism, one does something transcendent, more than this-worldly. I cannot overemphasize how remarkable is the combination of rational criticism and supernatural value attached to that criticism. We simply cannot understand Rabbinic Judaism without confronting the other-worldly context in which this so completely secular thinking goes forward. The claim is that in seeking reason and order, you serve God. But what are we to make of that claim? Does lucid thinking bring heavenly illumination? How can people suggest so?

Perhaps the best answer may be sought in this-worldly experience. Whence comes insight? Having put everything together in a logical and orderly way, we sometimes find ourselves immobilized. We know something, but we do not know what it means, what it suggests beyond itself. Then, sometimes, we catch an unexpected insight, and come in some mysterious way to a comprehension of a whole which exceeds the sum of its parts. And we cannot explain how we have seen what, in a single instant, stuns us by its ineluctable rightness, fittingness—by the unearned insight, the inexplicable understanding. For the rabbis that stunning moment of rational insight comes with *siyyata dishamaya*, "the help of heaven." The charisma imparted by the Rabbinic imagination to the brilliant man is not different in substance from the moral authority and spiritual dignity imparted by contemporary intellectuals to the great minds of the age. The profound honor to be paid to the intellectual paragons, the explorers of the unknown, the men and women of courage to doubt the accepted truths of the hour, is not much different from the deference shown by the disciple to the rabbi. So the religious experience of the rabbi and the secular experience of the intellectual differ not in quality. They gravely differ in the ways by which we explain and account for that experience. Still, in reflecting upon the commonalities of experience, we are enabled to enter into the curious mode of religiosity discovered within the Talmud.

Rabbinic Judaism divorced from its mythic context, its larger meanings for the construction of reality and the interpretation of life, is nothing else than a mere tradition. And a tradition perceived as traditional is also conceived as passed. But the Talmud, the central document of Rabbinic Judaism, understood as an expression of religion, as the statement of the inner world of saints, becomes a vivid alternative. For ultimate meanings are not bound to a particular place or time, and a way to the sacred, once discovered, remains forever open. What today is sought, and I think what is acutely required, is not what we already have, but what we realize we do not have: a mythic context for our being, a larger world of meanings for our private and individual existence. These have been found by seekers of mystic experience in the suppression of the intellect and the willful suspension of unbelief. Within the Talmud we are able to see them in the cultivation of the intellect and the criticism even of belief. The mystery of the Talmud and of the Judaism founded on it is its capacity to sanctify the one thing we do not propose to abandon, which is our capacity to doubt, our commitment to criticize, above all, the beautiful, reasoned, open-ended discourse created among contentious, learning men and women. The wonder of the Talmud is its tough-minded claims in behalf of the intellect as a mode of the sacred.

DISCUSSION

Smith—I didn't hear any method in this paper. This was not method, this was a sense of the sacredness of the intellect, and the reverence for reality which transcends oneself. Plus . . . a total intellectual integrity which would mean that one lived in accord with whatever one thought.

To reduce the rabbis to method would be to omit the spirit that animated them. Am I wrong?

Neusner—No. I agree with you.

Question—Do you see any correlation at all in the perspective of Judaism after the holocaust, between this intellectualizing and rationalizing of the tradition even in its political dimensions?

Neusner—. . . The history of Judaism is expressed around two poles: on the one side, concern for and response to historical events; on the other side, an effort to transcend events and transform Israel into a timeless community.

I think you see this most clearly in the early centuries of the Common Era, where you have a number of centuries of obsession with the nature and meaning of events expressed through apocalyptic, Messianic movements, etc.

I think the point and purpose of early Rabbinism is to respond by the construction of a new reality which is, so to speak, insulated from history, which will divert the Jews' attention away from historical events . . . .

So . . . you have these two polarities. In modern Judaism the immense changes which the Jewish people underwent, along with other peoples in the throes of modernization from the end of the 18th century onward, produced again a tremendous awareness of the meaning of events, of change, of the direction of history, and great concern for what it all meant, and produced therefore two major Messianic movements: Zionism and Reform Judaism. Taking opposite views of the Apocalypse and the Eschaton, in that order, both movements, in my view, have exhausted all that they have to say . . . . I don't think we will hear from Zionism or Reform Judaism something which we have not already heard.

You have this other angle of vision, namely, the sense that history is not the whole story, but there are eternities in time to be entered into, so to speak. That is my conception of what is central about Rabbinic Judaism.

Smith—I thought I heard from your presentation a *Weltanschauung*, and it seems to me, if the rabbis felt they were imitating God in their study, if they had a reverence for what they were doing, if the use of the intellect was a ritual . . . this does not seem to me a method in the sense that it's something you can pick up if you like it and drop it if you don't. Methods seem to be a choice.

I don't think anybody can choose as a plan of procedure, an ethos whereby he reveres the intellect of his colleague and his own and has a sense of the holiness of the procedure in which he's engaged.

Therefore I did not hear a method. Did I mishear you?

Neusner—No.

Question—How many scientists really question the validity of science, and how reasonable would it be in modern days to do so?

Neusner—Let me revise my description.

Rabbis cannot be represented as having stood completely outside the system in which they were doing their work. That would be a mode of skeptical thinking which I could not claim to find.

This skeptical mode represents an important point of difference between the modern intellectual who stands outside of all structures and the Rabbinic intellectual who is so radical and creative within his given structure.

V

THE PROBLEM OF SEMANTICS IN
THE STUDY OF RELIGION

Hans H. Penner

In this paper I will assume the premises and hypotheses developed in my first essay, entitled, "Creating a *Brahman*." Although the focus of our discussion will be on the particular problem of semantics in the study of religion it will continue to demonstrate the importance of theoretical considerations in our discipline. The discussion will also support my statement that the study of religion does not need unique theories.

We are all familiar with the debates about the autonomy of the study of religion. I know of no way of overcoming the claims and counterclaims except by showing that the arguments for an autonomous theory of religion cannot be sustained. A brief look at definitions of religion should make this clear. To say, for example, that religion is "ultimate concern" implies that an explanation of religion, assuming the definition is formally adequate, will be embedded in a theory regarding concerns. To assert that religion is a "belief system" implies an explanation of religion within some theory about beliefs.

If we assume that at some point we can state the theory we are using to explain religion it becomes obvious that such an explanation will be in the context of a theory about beliefs, concerns, values, and the like. That is to say, it is our theory about concerns and beliefs that explains religion; religion is a feature of concerns or beliefs.

The only exception I am aware of is an approach to religion which claims that it is *sui generis*, since the sacred reality which religions express is unique. I have already tried to discuss some of the problems in this approach and will only repeat that I cannot see how it can ever lead to the construction of a well-formed theory that can be tested. In any case, most studies of religion which assume this approach to religion soon return to beliefs, concerns, needs, and symbols which in turn take us back to at least a minimum theoretical framework which includes more than religion. What remains as the unique feature of religion involves our intuitions about the sacred. Now we may very well become interested in each other's intuitions but we must not confuse descriptions of our intuitions with explanations of religion.

Viewed in this way we can see why it is the case that our definitions can become first-order reductions for the construction of a theory. We may, for example, think that defining religion as a "belief system" will lead to a theory which is more adequate than others. The test, of course, will include both the formal validity of the theory and the empirical test of its adequacy and comprehensiveness. This does not imply that we have put an end to religion, academic departments of religion, or courses which specifically study religion. We need not enter the pragmatic and professional arguments for protecting the study of religion if we notice that in an analogous way neither chemistry nor biology has been abolished because of their use of theoretical physics.

My argument against the notion of a theoretically unique study of religion is, of course, a little premature. No one to my knowledge has presented us with such a theory. What we are given are statements of principle over which we can agree or disagree. When we review books, articles and reports on the study of religion, about the only thing everyone seems to agree upon is that the term "religion" does exist and that there are systems in the world which we can identify as "world religions." From a point which at first appears to have tacit consensus we soon find all sorts of disagreements on practically every issue that is raised with regard to the meaning of religion. The disagreements do not just involve the meaning of religious traditions, texts, myths, rituals, and symbols but also include disagreement about the term "religion." There are many who think we would be better off without the term, and this raises a new controversy about the best way to get rid of it. There are others who claim that the meaning of the term "religion" is indispensable only to find themselves embroiled in a controversy on the best way to explain the term. In the meantime, charges of "reductionist" and countercharges of "mystic" or "ontologist" blot the pages and pollute the air of discussions on religion.

Progress on the subject of semantics, which I consider to be central to our discipline, has been negligible. We have made great gains in accumulating vast collections of data but practically nothing has happened in the development of principles which could bring some order to the data. On a theoretical level our achievements seem to be inversely proportional to the significance of our subject.

What is the source of this misadventure? Who is to blame? Where do we look for help in order to make the necessary change? I think the source of our problem is the question regarding the meaning of religion. Regardless of which side of the aisle we are on, whether we think that a science of religion can be developed, or whether we are certain that it will never happen, clarification of the semantic problems we face will decide the issue. As far as the third question is concerned I think we may receive a great deal of help from recent developments in semantic theory within the field of linguistics. The remainder of this paper will attempt to show that there are some striking parallels between the development of semantics in general and approaches to the study of religion. My thesis will be that whether we are for or against the notion of a science of religion our position is determined by where we stand with regard to semantic theory in general.[1]

Scholars of religion who remain skeptical about solving the problem of meaning in religion are in good company. For the last 50 years the majority of linguists would have agreed. They would agree not because religion was uniquely mysterious but because semantics was ruled out of the scientific study of language. Most scholars in linguistics were very skeptical about the possibility of ever constructing a theory which would adequately explain the semantic component of language.

Ullmann has summed up the situation very nicely. In his introduction to the chapter on "meaning" he says:

> Meaning is one of the most ambiguous and most controversial terms in the theory of language. In *The Meaning of Meaning*, Ogden and Richards collected no less than sixteen different definitions of it—twenty-three if each subdivision is counted separately. Since then, many new uses, implicit or explicit, have been added to this formidable growth of ambiguity, and in the opinion of some scholars the term has become unusable for scientific purposes . . . . Most scholars, however, are reluctant to abandon such a fundamental term; they prefer to redefine it and to add various qualifications to it.[2]

The parallel between Ullmann's description of the linguists' problem with the term "meaning," and our problem with the term "religion" is quite interesting. The multiplicity of definitions, and the fact that it seems highly unlikely that we will ever reach universal agreement on the meaning of the term, has led many historians of religion to give up on the problem altogether.

In linguistics the problem of meaning was left behind. The study of language became equivalent to taxonomies of sound patterns and the analysis of phonemes and morphemes. There can be no doubt about the success of this kind of analysis. Phonology could tell us what the smallest units of the acoustical system of a language are, and this produced the phonetic system of a language. Morphology analyzed the smallest units of word structure, which in turn produced the minimal components of a grammatical system. And only recently the postulate of a deep structure provided us with the transformational rules which explained how it is possible to speak an indefinite number of sentences never uttered before based upon a finite morpho-phonetic system.

In spite of the success, the problem of meaning remained untouched; meaning escaped the analysis of language. Neither Saussure's question regarding how to go about describing the totality of a language nor Chomsky's revolution in the study of language in 1957 brought semantics into the study of language. This is not to say that linguists were unaware of the fact that morpho-phonetic analysis could not explain meaning. They knew that syntactic analysis of a language tells us that the sentence, "colourless green ideas sleep furiously," is grammatically correct. But they also knew that syntactic analysis could not tell us why the expression was meaningless. The grammar of the phrase, "the bill is large," could be explained but the ambiguity of the sentence was obviously not dependent upon syntactic differences. The ambiguity was dependent upon the different meanings of the term "bill." This stubborn problem led Chomsky, for example, to conclude in 1957 that grammar and semantics are autonomous and independent. The only problem with this solution is that it left semantics in the hands of *ad hoc* interpretations.

The implications of a division of language into two autonomous domains did not remain hidden for long. After making the observation that linguistics has suffered from a phonetic bias and the stress on observable data such as sound, Wallace Chafe drew the obvious conclusion:

> An easy conclusion to come to is that the satisfactory observation of meaning is impossible, that the best that can

be hoped for is the development of a theory of language with minimum reliance on such observation. This was, in fact, the conclusion reached by structural linguists, and the one which has influenced the main direction of syntacticism. If such a conclusion is inescapable, then language will continue to remain largely a mystery to us.[3]

If language precedes religion on a formal level, and I assume that it does, then Chafe's conclusion does not provide much joy for skeptics. For he is not saying that meaning will continue to remain a mystery, but that language itself will continue to remain a mystery. Chafe was not the only linguist who saw the implications of such an admission. The work of such scholars as Chomsky, Fodor, McCawley, Katz and Postal indicates that they are well on their way to constructing a theory of language which necessarily involves both syntactic and semantic rules. Once again, their theoretical work illustrates reduction at work, since if the theory is successful it will not only incorporate theories of the past but also explain an important feature of language that remains ineffable.

I also find the procedure for constructing such a theory quite helpful for my own reflections on the problem of meaning in religion. Katz states it very succinctly in the following way:

> If one believes, as I do, that the tragic history of semantics is instead a consequence of the failure to pursue a satis-factory approach to understanding meaning, he has no more nor less to do than construct a theory that uses the concept of meaning to reveal underlying uniformities in language and to show how semantic phenomena reduce to them. It would be a mistake to believe that at this stage one can silence the skeptic in any other way. Advancing philosophical arguments against the principles on which skepticism rests would just renew old debates. The only convincing argument consists in showing that the concept of meaning provides the basis for a theory that successfully accounts for semantic facts and in showing that without this concept no such basis exists.[4]

As far as I can tell the semantic problem of religion presents us with a situation represented by linguistics a few years ago. With one important exception, which I shall return to in a moment, the problem of meaning in religion has been sidestepped. If such a situation is inescapable, then we can also conclude that religion will continue to remain largely a mystery to us. Of course, we are not entirely at fault; after all, we are not professionals in the field of semantics. Even if we assumed that religion must be studied in a wider theoretical context, linguistics until a few years ago would have offered us very little help on the problem of meaning. Nevertheless, I do think that our growing professionalism and tacit agreement regarding the ineffability of meaning helped us kick the problem of meaning to the man upstairs.

We are all familiar with the assertion that the "essential" meaning of religion is its "vertical dimension" which is not open to empirical analysis. Another version of this principle is that the study of religion, the history of religions, is descriptive not normative. In other words, the truth conditions of religious language, a feature of semantics, are not open to us. They must, instead, be placed in the hands of theologians, metaphysicians, or religious philosophers. This skepticism with regard to the meaning of religion has led us into situations which has led us into situations which are quite perplexing. For example, the moment a historian of religions tries to explain the meaning of religion he is called a theologian, ontologist, or mystic. Now this is apparently a bad thing; but then we are told that it is exactly these kind of people that hold the key to the meaning of religion in a particular religious tradition. For some reason, which is never disclosed, we are to listen to mystics and ontologists in a particular religion for what is normative, but not to others of a similar persuasion outside that tradition. And then when all of the normative assertions face us head on we move to the inevitable conclusion that the norms or principles of meaning are after all ethno- or religio-centric. In other words, religious relativism leads to the conclusion that the syntax of religion is independent from the semantics of religion.

Anyone familiar with the history of religions will agree, I think, that what I have just described can be found in studies of religion from Bleeker to van der Leeuw, and from Wach to Baird. Once the division of labor was well-founded we went on to classify, typologize and describe the history of religions in a variety of ways. If we keep the parallel of linguistics in mind, it is certainly true that we did not develop anything near the morpho-phonetic analysis which became so successful in the study of language. Nevertheless, we do have some excellent historical and typological studies of religion. But we have also recognized in a variety of ways that historical and typological studies of religion are not equivalent to the meaning of religion, and that is the semantic problem we face. Using the parallel from linguistics once again, most of us are aware of the fact that a summary, or an accumulation of a religious tradition does not constitute the meaning of a religion.

Perhaps it would be wise to move more slowly at this point because it may not be evident that most of us are aware of the fact that a description of a religious tradition is not equivalent to the meaning of a religion. The distinction which I am following comes from Saussure's insistence that an analysis of language will always fail if we do not separate diachronic from synchronic features of language. I am assuming that the same distinction holds for religion. When we confuse these important distinctions it often appears as if the study of the development of a religion will produce its meaning, that the surface structure will yield the deep structure of a religion. But a moment's reflection should teach us that this is impossible. It would mean that regardless of where we stopped our diachronic or surface analysis we would never reach a point where we could speak of the meaning of religion for the simple reason that its history continues. In short, the sum of a religious tradition even if we could conceive of it is not equivalent to the meaning of religion. To identify the history of a religion with the meaning of religion would be analogous to an attempt at painting a portrait from photographs of a person taken at various times in life from infancy to old age. The notion of structure as a system of transformational rules which generate both syntactic and semantic units which explain surface structure is a consequence of the discovery that we must distinguish between the history of a language or a religion and its synchronic structure. From this point of view the meaning of religion cannot be the summation of its history, but will be found in the totality of the sense its lexical units provide within a structure.

Historians and phenomenologists of religion are not alone in separating meaning from the analysis of religion. If we leave aside the logical problems of functional explanations we can see that functional approaches to religion are in basic agreement with this separation. Malinowski made the separation a basic principle when he said that we must proceed to study the function of cults and creeds because we cannot define them by their objects. With this principle in hand functionalists did indeed proceed to tell us about the consequences of religious language and behavior for the needs of individuals and society. And with few exceptions, Evans-Pritchard for one, they soon forgot that their scientific approach excluded a fundamental feature of religion: its object.

The history of functionalism provides ample evidence on the exclusion of the object of creed and cult. Attempts to correct this fault have often led to the assertion that the function of religion *is* its meaning, religion is nothing but a symbolic representation of society. This principle of meaning can be tested. If we apply it we find that it is quite inadequate. In fact, no functionalist from Durkheim to Spiro has been able to show that religious language and behavior is "synonymous," or equivalent to the empirical facts of society. In fact if Lévi-Strauss has taught us anything, it is the important discovery that religious language is often the converse, or "antonymous," to the facts of society.

The semantic problem we face in both phenomenological and functional approaches to religion can be summed up very nicely with a remark by Quine on the identical problem in linguistics:

> Pending a satisfactory explanation of the notion of meaning, linguists in semantic fields are in the situation of not knowing what they are talking about. This is not an untenable situation. Ancient astronomers knew the movements of the planets remarkably well without knowing what sort of things the planets were. But it is a theoretically unsatisfactory situation, as the more theoretically-minded among linguists are painfully aware.[5]

Relief from the pain was brought about by a very important shift in emphasis. We can solve the semantic problem if we can reduce the notion of meaning to a theory of reference. According to this well-known solution to our problem, if we want to explain the meaning of religion we must explain it by showing what religion refers to. This theoretical shift is the exception I mentioned when I stated that the problem of semantics has been sidestepped in the study of religion.

Before reflecting on the consequences of this important shift in emphasis I want to dwell for a moment on my assertion that the semantic problem can be solved if we can reduce meaning to a theory of reference. The statement illustrates why historians of religions should not be threatened by the term "reduction." When we equate meaning with reference in our attempt to solve semantic problems in religion it is clear that we have not dissolved or splintered the data into nothingness. In brief, we have not explained the data away. Meaning is a theoretical term, a term embedded in a theory which seeks to explain what things mean, or what sense they have. Reference is another theoretical term, embedded in a second theory. Now if we can show that reference is equivalent to meaning we can reduce theories of meaning to a theory of reference in order to explain our data as well as solve problems which the reduced theory could not solve.

There is a second feature in the operation of theoretical reduction which is just as important as the one just described. The history of science shows us that the process of theoretical reduction is open-ended. The possibility of reduction not only allows us to uncover new problems and discoveries. Reduction is at the very core of the continuing development of our knowledge of the world and this obviously includes the history of religions.

With few exceptions, historians of religion have not concerned themselves with the theoretical complexities of their explanations of religion. Threatened by reduction we have also been threatened by the construction of theories. Our anti-reductionist claims could be viewed as ironic were it not for the fact that we have unwittingly assumed a theoretical reduction in our use of reference as an explanation of the meaning of religion.

The reasons why we have resisted theoretical reduction need not be entered into here. All we need to see is that the consequences of our opposition to theoretical construction have led us into the misconception that when we speak about the reference of religion we are saying something that is simple and direct. What we fail to realize, however, is that when we say "religion points to the sacred," or that the object of religion is this or that, we are not making simple statements of fact. The question, "What is the meaning of religion?", or, "What is the reference of religion?" is not equivalent to "Where is the University of Iowa?" Katz states the misconception in the following way:

> The question, "What is meaning?" does *not* admit of a direct "this or that" answer; its answer is instead a whole theory. It is not a question like "What is the capital of France?", "When did Einstein retire?", "Where is Tasmania?" because it is not merely a request for an isolated fact, a request which can be answered simply and directly. Rather, it is a theoretical question, like, "What is matter?", "What is electricity?", "What is light?".[6]

Our acquaintance with the study of religion should make it obvious that debates between phenomenologists and functionalists, for example, are not based upon a theoretical disagreement. Most phenomenologists and historians of religion are quite tolerant of functionalism. All we need is an agreement that religion does not simply refer to the satisfaction of needs but also includes some reference to the sacred, to ultimate reality or ultimate concern. What we need, in other words, is some consensus on the point that religion does not simply refer to one thing, it is more complex than that. Religion is similar to the word "board," which does not simply refer to a thin wooden plank, but also to a table, food service and persons who direct a corporation. Our problem, according to phenomenologists, is that functionalists are like Oliver Twist, who, when he was told by Bumble to bow to the "board," "seeing no 'board' but the table, fortunately bowed to that."[7] And the functionalist answers this criticism by saying that he is committed to empirical principles and will never bow to anything he cannot see.

The point of this characterization is that when we do face the problem of semantics we usually solve it by equating meaning with reference. The fact that this shift is not a simple matter of fact can be seen in the complex debates which have gone on with regard to the adequacy of the reduction of meaning to reference. It has involved logicians, philosophers of language, and linguists in a discussion of such topics as intensional and extensional definitions, the relation between analytic and synthetic propositions, and the problem of synonymy.

Our lack of professional competence to enter into such discussions should not prevent us from at least becoming familiar with a theory which we are implicitly assuming. According to Katz, the equation of meaning with reference

> says that we should construct a theory based upon the principle that the meaning of an expression is the entity, class of entities, event, class of events, and so on that the expression names (refers to, denotes, designates). Accordingly, the meaning of "Bertrand Russell" is the man named, the meaning of "men" is the class of adult male humans, the meaning of "Columbus' discovery of America" is the historic event of 1492, and so forth. The attraction of this equation seems to be that it brings meaning out into the open, making it something no more mysterious than the things, persons, places and events of daily life.[8]

The pervasiveness of this theory in the study of religion will become evident when we remember that long ago it was simply assumed that the referent of religion was nature itself. Agni means fire, Varuna means moon, and other deities and spirits referred to the sun, water, lightening, or corn. Our forefathers never did solve the problem of why it was the case that uncivilized people failed to realize that they were misusing language. But they did notice that if they attached evolutionary theory to reference it became clear that the more advanced cultures became the more abstract the religious reference. Instead of referring to such simple objects as the sun, moon and stars, gods and goddesses in advanced cultures referred to justice, virtue, love, desire, and goodness. And finally at the height of the development of religion gods referred to potentiality, power, creativity, and even being-itself.

It was not prolonged reflection on the adequacy of a theory of reference that shook us out of this magnificent explanation of religion. It was the sudden recognition that the evolutionary schema we had attached to referential theory contradicted the liberal-minded assumption that all men are equal both rationally and morally. Tylor, Frazer, and Lévy-Bruhl were not just wrong about religion, they were ethnocentric ideologists. And so we dropped the evolutionary schema, got out of our ethnocentric armchairs, and went into the field where we could see that religion does not refer to nature, ethics, or metaphysics but in actual fact to the social system of which it is a part. Religion referred to needs, to instincts which were repressed, or to peak experiences in a culture or person.

Phenomenologists of religion, as we have already noted, agree in principle that reference is meaning. However, they remained unsatisfied with the kinds of things, events, and classes of things and events, which everyone else was saying religion referred to. Phenomenologists of religion had put their finger on a significant problem in spite of the fact that both functionalists and historicists had good reasons to remain skeptical about their solution.

Phenomenologists of religion solved the problem by asserting that religion refers to the sacred, to a reality that cannot be described as an event, a thing, or a class of events. In other words, whatever it was that religion referred to it was not a thing; the sacred is no thing but a transcendent reality. And since it is the case that both phenomenologists and historians of religion continue to refuse to explicate this reality, for fear of becoming normative, they have landed in what can be described as pan-symbolism. But their insistence on the principle that meaning is reference implies that pan-symbolism is fictionalism. Left without a specifiable referent we compared, classified, and typed religious traditions and symbols. Caught between fictionalism on the one hand, and functionalism on the other, many of us turned out typologies and histories into the referent of religion without realizing that we were now going around in circles.

It would be rather reckless to assert that the solution to our problem involves the elimination of the term "reference." It is obvious that there are many words and expressions in every language which refer to an object. Our problem is a theoretical one, it involves the adequacy of reducing meaning to reference, or simply assuming that meaning is reference.

Consensus on the principle of reference, it seems, never led us to ask why it is the case that we could not reach any agreement on what it is that religion refers to. This situation led me to ask myself whether there was a referent to religion. What if the phenomenologists were right for the wrong reasons? Perhaps religion does not refer to anything because anything does not refer! What were the alternatives? Function-alism was clearly out because it not only assumes that meaning is reference but also has problems with the logic of its explanation. Behaviorism was not an option after the devastating critique of Chomsky, and besides, it too assumed that meaning is reference. There seemed to be one alternative left, and that was structuralism.

If Chomsky provided us with a revolution in linguistics, Lévi-Strauss surely produced one in anthropology. At the heart of his work we find the postulate that the meaning of myth, for example, is equivalent to its structure, and that the structure of myth is not identical with its surface features. In other words, he was bold enough to assert that both referential theory and empiricism are inadequate when it comes to the task of explaining myths. He then went on to show that it is also a mistake to explain totems by reference to their social significance. Instead of assuming that totems are "good to eat" we should think of them as "good to think." For if it is the case that the significance, that is, the meaning, of a totem is its social value how do we go about explaining the social value of sleep totems, wind totems, and vomit totems?

For some reason which I cannot explain, historians of religions remained rather neutral when this revolution broke out. This was certainly not the case in anthropology. The first reaction, especially from the British side of the discipline, was almost hysterical. Anyone reading Mary Douglas' critique of "The Story of Asdiwal" cannot help but notice that Lévi-Strauss must have hit a very vulnerable spot in functionalism in order to arouse such wrath.[9]

The basic criticism which has been levelled against Lévi-Strauss is that it is not formal enough! Many of us would certainly agree with his criticism of explanations of culture which are based upon "affectivity," or other obscure terms such as "sacred" or "transcend-ence." Such explanations do indeed lose sight of the principle that "what is refractory to explanation is *ipso facto* unsuitable for use in explanation."[10] What is lacking in the work of Lévi-Strauss is a well-formed theory which we can follow. Without such a theory it becomes exceedingly difficult to follow his technique in order to find out whether it is the case that the special feature of myth is mediating contradictions.

It is important to remember that contradiction plays a crucial function in Lévi-Strauss' brand of structural analysis. Although I cannot fully document my argument here I do want to submit that the weakness of his approach is due to the fact that his notion of structure is dependent upon older theories of linguistics which emphasized syntax to the exclusion of semantics. Lévi-Strauss is not overly concerned with the problems of semantics. What he looks for are units that are similar to morphemes. What I find odd is that he has borrowed a semantic term, contradiction, to explain the syntax of myth. If semantics is not his primary concern, and if his notion of structure is equivalent to syntactic analysis, we will need an explanation for the use of contradiction as the key to the structural analysis of myth. What we will need is an adequate theory of semantics which will place the semantic feature of contradiction in its proper setting. Without such a theory I think that Lévi-Strauss's approach will continue to appear to be an *ad hoc* application of the word "contradiction."

It is only recently that scholars have attempted to formalize such a theory. The work by Jerrold Katz, for example, is a good indication of the new directions which are being taken in the formalization of a theory of semantics. His classic article, written together with Fodor, entitled, "The Structure of a Semantic Theory," was primarily responsible for the introduction of a semantic component in contemporary structural linguistics.[11]

According to Katz, a well-formed theory of semantics must answer the following kinds of question: What is sameness of meaning? What are similarity and difference of meaning? What are meaningfulness and meaninglessness? What is multiplicity or ambiguity of meaning? What is truth by virtue of meaning? He goes on to state that these kinds of questions lead to subquestions such as: what is synonymy, semantic similarity, antonymy, superordination, ambiguity, redundancy, and the like.[12]

After constructing a provisional list of questions which are directly related to semantics, Katz says that,

> An answer to "What is meaning?" therefore, cannot be given merely by equating the meaning of a linguistic construction with say, what it names or refers to, or with dispositions according to which it is used correctly, or with the mental idea for which it is the sensible external sign, or with the eliciting and controlling of stimuli that produce it as a verbal response, or with the eternal Platonic archetype for which it stands.[13]

Katz argues quite correctly, I believe, that each of the above principles must be developed into a well-formed theory which will explicate the questions which semantics raises. And the test for any of the above principles is its capacity to explain the semantic phenomena involved in the basic questions which arise when we ask, "What is meaning?"

We need not go into the complex syntactic and semantic components of a transformational theory of semantics in order to see the implications of Katz' argument. Following the criteria that Katz has given us the equation of meaning with reference is the first principle which fails. It fails simply because, as Frege showed long ago, it cannot explain the semantic phenomena of synonymy.

If we take reference to mean those things to which an expression refers, then as Frege pointed out, such nonsynonymous phrases as "the evening star" and "the morning star" are falsely explained as synonymous. By extension, if the meaning of all religious expressions refers to the satisfaction of social or psychological needs, then such nonsynonymous religious statements as, "He who has lost all hope rests content" and "For we are saved by hope" are synonymous. Similarly, if we take the sacred as that to which all and only those expressions which are religious refer, then all religious expressions such as "There is no god but Allah," "O Savitri, grant us knowledge," and "The Tao that can be expressed in words is not the eternal Tao" are synonymous.

When we look at the semantic problems in religion from this position it becomes obvious that a great deal of our time has been spent on problems arising from the simple equation of meaning with reference. But, the basic question is theoretical: is the principle of reference adequate for a theory of meaning? From this very brief analysis, I think the answer to that question is no. And if scholars in linguistics are now working towards the construction of a theory of semantics which agrees with this conclusion we have come a long way from the days when religion was talked about as nonsense because religious expressions do not entail an empirical referent.

A well-formed theory of meaning will, I am certain, provide us with the proper framework for the study of religion. A theory of religion, if this is desired, will become a subdivision of semantic theory. It may very well be the case that as the answers to semantic questions are worked out we will find that religious expressions exhibit peculiar or special semantic features as a subsystem of syntactic and semantic structures in general. At the moment this is only a guess, for the work remains to be done.

In conclusion I would like to point out, very briefly, that semantics also holds the key to another problem in the study of religion. It is the difficult problem of the translatability of world religions, or more succinctly, the inter-translatability of religious languages. The obvious extension of this problem involves the possibility of translating religious texts from one language into another.

Once again linguists as well as historians of religions are divided on this issue. There are those who would claim, following Sapir and Whorf, that although there may be semantic effability intra-linguistically, languages are ineffable inter-linguistically. There are others, following Frege, Searles, and Katz who postulate that all languages are effable in principle. That is to say, language is not only capable of expressing thought, but all languages are also inter-translatable.

Now this problem will not be solved by a division of this seminar into two camps and a quick trip to the library. For I am sure that both sides would find texts that they could argue are excellent translations, or, very poor translations. The reason that this problem will not be settled this way is because the issues involved are not simply empirical issues. As Katz has pointed out:

> Rather there is a serious conceptual problem involved as well, that is, there is the problem of specifying just what properties of sentences must be preserved in translation. Without a solution to this problem, we have no way to judge what would count as a real counterexample to a claim that one sentence is a translation of another. But the set of properties with respect to which we determine whether a sentence from one language has the same literal meaning as a sentence from another is exactly what determines sameness of meaning in general.[14]

I have now reached the end of my reflections on the problem of semantics in religion. Of all the questions which come to mind, one stands out rather clearly: what if it is the case that a well-formed theory of semantics cannot be constructed? What then? Well, for one thing we will have learned a great deal. We will have learned, for example, that chunks of history, as chunks of sound patterns, will not serve as a substitute for our failure. Furthermore, although it will be disappointing for rationalists to admit that the skeptics were right, we will be able to comprehend more adequately why it is the case that religion in particular and culture in general remain incomprehensible to us. I remain optimistic, fully aware that optimism is no substitute for hard work.

DISCUSSION

Question—Why should we be persuaded any more that structure is meaning than that reference is meaning?

Penner—It's not a matter of being persuaded that structure is meaning.

In the study of religion, you run into a basic problem. You seem to disagree with a lot of other people and when you get together, even though you agree on the basic premise, that meaning is reference, you can't agree on what it refers to.

Who is to blame? The reductionists, the mystics? That's not the solution. There's something wrong with the premise. It seems to me every discovery has reflected on that—maybe there's something wrong with the premise . . . .

Question—It seems you fall back into the reference theory by making what appears to be an implicit assumption that structure is that to which meaning refers.

Penner—Meaning doesn't refer to structure. Meaning is a semantic component *in* the structure, along with syntax. Otherwise we can't explain why it is that a statement is semantically meaningless but syntactically correct.

Question—You said . . . that what you were really looking for is something that could explain the totality of religion. That's where I see you falling back into the reference theory.

Penner—I want to see if I can contribute, in the history of religions, something to the ongoing revolution that has taken place. I don't want to isolate myself anymore.

I'm *in* that stream. I want to contribute something to it. I think the significance of my subject matter *has* something to contribute to that. That to me is the humanities.

What I want now is a description. I want to postulate a theory, to ask the question, "Is it possible to explicate the totality of meaning, or the totality of a religious system?"

If I follow this, I have to do two things. I can't leave syntax out; I have to have syntactic rules and semantic rules in religion in order to explain religion, if I follow the analogy of linguists . . . .

VI

IS THE COMPARATIVE STUDY OF RELIGIONS POSSIBLE?
PANEL DISCUSSION

Smith, Neusner, Penner

The Panel Discussion proceeded with each participant addressing himself to the question as to whether the comparative study of religions was possible. But the intention of the panel was to give the participants, having heard and reacted to each other's presentations, an opportunity to address themselves to what they considered to be the crucial issues which divided them or which they shared. This being the case the discussion moved quickly to a consideration of certain issues in the study of religion.

Neusner—My answer to the question is that it is not only possible, but it's indispensable. Of the three of us, I think I'm the one that concentrates most narrowly on a specific tradition and draws most eclectically on what I can learn from other fields. I can't understand my own material without knowing the choices—how things *could* have been—the choices that people are making among many which presumably are before them . . . . I gain a perspective on my data, therefore, by learning about other religions . . . .

The methods I'm working out in the study of the particular problems I want to solve, are borrowed, quite shamelessly, from New Testament scholarship, [and] to a lesser degree from Patristic scholarship, which I know far less well, although it interests me as much . . . .

I would like to give one concrete example of something that I learned
in this [symposium] which has stunned me . . . .

Prof. Penner described the [upanayana] ritual, and posed as his
problem, the interpretation of the ritual. And I listened with fascination
and I asked myself the question: In the data of Judaism in its Rabbinic
phase, which is [from the 1st to] the 17th or 18th century, could I offer
Prof. Penner a problem for interpretation? Do I have a ritual of such
detail, which I could say, here is a problem for your method . . . .
The answer [is] . . . no. That is to say, in the Judaism which we know
over the past 19 centuries, with some exceptions, it would be virtually
impossible to say, "This is something people do, this is a rite of passage."

I'll give you some examples:

The rite of passage from childhood to maturity, the *bar mitzvah*,
which everyone knows about . . . . The boy is called to say a blessing
before the reading of the Torah in the synagogue. The walking around
and so forth just doesn't exist.

The marriage rite consists of saying words. Now it is true that in
what we're going to have to call folk religion, there are rites associated
with the marriage, such as the walking around by the bride of the groom
seven times; the performance of the ceremony under the open sky, with
an intervening canopy; and other things which would be fraught with
meaning for the historian of religion, or the anthropologist, and so on.
I haven't got very much to ask. And the reason is, that all of our rites
and rituals are submerged in words—blessings, things one says; one
doesn't *do* very much.

I'll give you the example which bothered me the past 10 days:
We had the Passover Seder, and I have young children . . . and so I'm
very alert to doing things which my children will understand. And you
would think, what could be more vivid for a child or an adult than the
symbolism of the Seder? You have a plate on the table, and there are
various substances in the plate . . . .

When one comes to what one actually *does* at the Seder, and I
say, Prof. Penner, interpret for me, I have to give him a *book*! And
what bothers me is that the symbols on the table are virtually ignored
by the central word-formulae of the Passover service, until at the very
end you point to the *matzah*, and say what's it all about; to the bitter
herbs and say, what is this all about. It isn't saying anything to the
people, so they insert a little *pericope* at the end explaining the things
which we have carefully and sedulously ignored. Not only so, but not
all of the symbols, if you want to call them that, on the Seder plate,
are ever even referred to. What do you do with the lamb bone? What do
you do with the hard-boiled egg? And the parsley? A fertility rite? Of
course it's a fertility rite. What do the rabbis do who stand behind our
ceremony? The rite is preserved; the symbols are all on the table, and
then we act as if they're not there. So I learned something which irritated
me no end, and that is that Rabbinism by its imposition of the rite of
study has de-ritualized all other aspects of Judaism, as far as I'm able to
tell. And this is what the . . . intellectuals are all about. Fair enough? We
reduce it all to words. I think that in the comparative study of religions,

if you accept my picture of Judaism and Rabbinism, . . . you're going to have to say that we have paid a heavy price. And you're going to have all these . . . subterranean explosions which are going to try to re-naturalize the Judaic life cycle, . . . this is my appropriation of Richard Rubenstein's views in this regard.

I'll give you one final example: . . . Look at the Yom Kippur liturgy. What are we supposed to do on Yom Kippur? You get a very elaborate picture in Leviticus of a very, very elaborate ceremony, a sacrifice . . . . What do we do in the synagogue? On the afternoon of Yom Kippur, we read about what they *used* to do in the temple. And somehow I think that the tradition has, with all of its richness, lost something by the verbalization of all of the inherent and symbolic structure of pre-Rabbinic Judaism. So, this is by way of suggesting . . . how all these different angles of vision correct the distortion in the glasses of the person who studies primarily a single tradition . . . .

My last point is . . . university people. To me this is what university means. We all share part of the common task, and I for one, even though people think we're in crisis, . . . can't think of any other place I'd rather be than right where I am, or anything I'd rather do than what I'm doing. And I suspect that for most people the same can be said.

Smith—It is almost disappointing how closely Prof. Neusner and I converge at times! I seem to have little to disagree with, both in his opening and closing things especially.

To the question, is the comparative study of religion possible, my answer is yes.

Let me develop one thought which may land us in some clarification.

One of the things that interests me greatly in the comparative study of religion is India. There religious diversity as an issue, of course, is central. In the Hindu case, . . . the tradition is, of course, enormously varied. One striking thing about the Hindu [tradition] is its complexity. Over against that you have the Islamic; the more you look at it, the more elaborate it turns out to be, yet in principle it is simple. It is a system. It aims at being systematic, and it achieves its aim reasonably well. So one has here in India two radically different types of system: diversity on the one hand, an aspiration which leads to a kind of monolithic but coherent system, on the other.

There is the further point that to simplify the Hindu complex, the key notion for understanding is certainly that of symbol; each item is symbolic and almost everything he [the Hindu] does is symbolic of something; whereas the Islamic is aniconic, it is iconoclast, it has spent 1400 years smashing symbols. To understand the religious life of mankind, I think one has to understand both symbolism on the one hand and iconoclasm on the other.

Now, fascinating in this is that in the Islamic case the whole system is symbolic. It provides a *Weltanschauung*, a coherent frame through which one looks at the world. The comparative study of religion has made an enormous amount of progress in the last 100 years or so in coming to some kind of recognition of the role of symbols in religious life. But what we've not yet done, on the same level of competence, is to come to terms with a total system that operates symbolically. Not one of which the individual parts are symbolic, but the whole thing. And science, I think, is one of these. Western secular liberalism is of that type, and so on. There are other total *Weltan-schauungen* that are more like the Islamic than the Hindu or the Indian.

I like to think of myself as having made some progress towards understanding first of all the Islamic, on which I spent some years, more recently Hindu and Buddhist, and also my own Christian background, all of which I can claim to understand better now than I did 25 years ago. That cheers me. And I also am in some sense not merely heir to, but a committed devoted member of the classical rational humanist tradition in the Western world. I participate with a good deal of concentration in that.

I like to think that though a Christian and a Western liberal, . . . I have to some extent transcended the limitations of these two, insofar as they have limitations, and can now claim to participate intellectually not only in them but also in Islamic, Buddhist, Hindu outlooks, and I think I even understand the Jewish in a way which is probably true of everybody else here, too. It is distinctive of the modern world that we are to some degree not only informed about, but exposed to and sensitive to, the visions of these groups.

There is, however, a modern sect among us to which I am an outsider. Of it Hans Penner, I think, is a consecrated member.

I do not understand the recent (and I stress that) . . . Western . . . scientific, secular theorizing. This is a sect of which I'm not a member, and whose attractiveness to me is very small. I probably ought to, and I came here hoping, that I might expand my horizons to include also it in my sympathies; and I said on Monday night[1] that surely I'm wrong in my feeling that the methodological gambit here is in some sense threatening.

Listening to Hans Penner's two papers, and especially today's,[2] I have the feeling that I wasn't so wrong.

I thought perhaps I had really misunderstood what methodology was all about. He has somewhat persuaded me that I got it right. I still don't like it.

I've long maintained that . . . one of the most striking, significant, and precious things that any two religious systems could have in common would be a clear and mutually agreed understanding of their differences. I've been struggling very hard to see if I could formulate where we differ.

First of all, do we in fact differ? Have I been wrong in thinking that something quite different is going on here? He has rather persuaded me that yes, we do differ. There really is a basic divergence.

Let me see if I can formulate such a difference, and ask him, and you, to comment on my attempt to articulate the divergence as I see it.

The first point would certainly be my . . . personalism, my really very profound sense . . . that we as students are human beings and . . .

other people [whose religious life] we are studying are also human beings . . . . This is the most important factor at issue here . . . . The study of religion is primarily the understanding of persons, in a sense like ourselves, in another sense, not like ourselves. But I certainly am on the side of the greater importance of the fact that they are like ourselves.

And I feel that meaning inheres, resides in, is located in, that the locus of meaning is, persons. And I think that most of the problems of semantics which Prof. Penner dealt with stem from the almost refusal of the semanticists to take account of the fact that meaning is located in persons. I have never thought that meaning is reference. And the historians of religion whom I find rich have not thought this. So that a great deal of his paper seemed to me not pertaining to the things with which I am primarily concerned. I really was struck, Prof. Penner, by the fact that you didn't quote Eliade: you quoted Chomsky and Katz, and other Westerners, Lévi-Strauss, and so on, but not Streng on the Buddhists, or Fazlur Rahman on the Muslims, or Edward Dimock on the Hindus, or Neusner on the Jews, and so on, the people who have in fact in our field tried to explain the meaning of Jewish, Islamic, Buddhist, Hindu life.

That meaning, I claim, lies in persons.

The scientific enterprise, as I understand it, is deliberately, successfully, an attempt to de-personalize. It strains, struggles, strives to construct statements whose meaning and whose truth will be independent of the person who makes them, that will be interchangeable among everybody concerned. And this de-personalization works spectacularly well in the understanding of molecular chemistry and spectacularly badly in the understanding of human life.

So that, I think, is one place where we differ: on the centrality of the personal in the understanding of religion.

The second point where perhaps we differ: I found you [Prof. Penner] used the term "explain religion" many times, which I think I would never do. I use the word "understand." You talked about "understanding and explaining," I of "knowing and understanding"; and I translated "know" by *connaître* rather than *savoir*, by *kennen* rather than *wissen* and so on.

I got the impression . . . that the interest here is to provide a *theory* of religion. Now I am not aiming at a theory of religion. I'm aiming at an understanding of religious people, and of religion, too, if you like. I'm pretty sure that understanding cannot be formulated in words that can be de-personalized in the sense of everybody taking them, whoever he be. If I arrive at an understanding of anything, or my students do, or somebody who writes a book does—I read his book in the hopes that I as a person will see, will understand . . . . Somehow within his own person each student or scholar will grow . . . he will become the kind of person who now understands. Jewish, Rabbinic, study, for instance: I think I now understand this better than I did last week. I don't have a theory about it, I'm just a different person, and I'm not aiming at a theory, though I certainly applaud the fact that the

author is capable of saying what he understands in words that communicate to me. This is splendid.

That then would be my second point: that the goal at which I
think our study is aiming is not the construction of any universal
theory. Given the history of human affairs, it seems to me evident that
the verbalizations of our understandings are culture bound. I admit
that the ecumenists are moving toward statements that will be more
universally acceptable, intelligible. But I do not think that they will be
statements taken from that small sect of the recent West: secular
academic and scientific. The humanist strikes me as much more
promising, potentially.

Well, that's my attempt. I would like to know if you think I have
at all articulated [the divergences].

Penner—Well, I think you've done very well . . . .

We all seem to agree on the question we are here to reflect on, and
I would want to agree with the two of you that the question, is a
comparison possible, is not a question we can escape. It's not a question
of can we or can't we; we don't have any choice. The moment I read
Jacob Neusner or Wilfred Cantwell Smith on Islam I'm reading
translations and I'm already comparing—it's just put in English. Your
work is put in English from other kinds of translations, so the comparison has already taken place. What we have to do then is test the
comparison. Because when we compare we're looking for similarities
and differences, even if it's in the translation of a text. We can go a step
higher and talk about comparisons between religious traditions, for
example, and we're again asking the question of similarities and
differences. Those are semantic terms . . . .

This assumes the effability principle of language—I think languages
are not only inter- but intra-linguistically translatable. I know very well,
again, that there is disagreement on that by historians of religion . . . And
here again I think the questions do come down to semantic issues, as to
what we mean by similarity and difference and what the properties of
sameness are before we can get to the point of what we're talking about
or where we disagree. That area has to be uncovered more fully.

Winch . . . is after the same kind of problem. Students often tell
me, "You talk about Hinduism or *nirvana*, but unless you experience
that you don't know what you're talking about." . . .

I think Winch has a proper reply to that—that's almost like
saying linguistically that unless I am a native speaker of language B, I
don't understand that language. But when I become a native speaker of
language B, I have a problem speaking languages A, C, E, and F. Things
have just shifted. So we have to work out ways to articulate this
problem as far as possible.

I think the answer to the question is definitely yes. It's a
necessity—we don't have any choice in it. It's just a matter of how we
articulate the problems.

On the sectarian problem—I'm not quite sure how to handle that
one. I'm not particularly depressed that I'm in a sect—the sect may be
right. There are a lot of things I don't like, but what I don't like may

be true. That's one of the reasons why I have to continue to investigate them.

I think where we differ is that I think it *is* the case that we can approach what I would call your [Smith's] position of personalism and I would translate that again . . . as the performance of a religious act, which can be called a speech act. That's certainly an area of investigation. When someone performs a language, that's something I can investigate. But I don't know whether I want to translate that into the only alternative, because obviously, when I speak I'm speaking a language and that's why I want to go back to constructing what the possibilities are for that. I don't see how I can start with a person speaking a language, or performing a ritual, or repeating a myth or whatever else it may be . . . .

It is quite the case that I did not *cite* anyone in the paper directly . . . . What I will have to show is that your [Smith's] *The Meaning and End of Religion* assumes a referential theory of language and I must also show that almost every historical religion I've come across assumes that position.

Whether the reference is history, whether it's function, whether it's the sacred, is irrelevant to me. What I'm interested in at the moment is the *use* of reference. I think the task will now be upon me to show that that's the case.

Smith—The notion of reference, I take it, is that the word "sun" means that object up in the sky.

Penner—That's one example of it. It could also mean that the meaning of a religion is its historical, cumulative, tradition . . . .

Smith—But I'm claiming that the meaning of the word "sun" is not up in the sky, it's in a person.

Penner—I just simply don't understand that.

Smith— . . . I think it's important, because I feel very strongly that to locate meaning anywhere else than in persons is part of the movement to de-personalize modern society, which is making such havoc of our lives.

Penner—I don't understand that one either . . . . You're going to chop off the one or the other—persons, individuals, certainly speak languages, utter religious sentences, have religious experiences, and so forth. But it's because of something else that this is the case. Surely the meaning of "sun" is so and so, or the meaning of "sun" means something, but it's not inside me somewhere. Inside me where? In my head? In my heart? It's in the language that was given me. I had no choice.

Smith—I think it's in your heart, in your head, in the heart and head of your parents who taught you English.

Penner—That's exactly it. It was given to me.

Neusner—That's where you [Smith] have to emerge from a narrow subjectivity.

Smith —I'm not a narrow subjectivist. I'm neither narrow nor subjectivist. I'm personalist.

Penner—It's the same thing.

Smith—No, it's not. This is the point. My goal is a corporate self-consciousness which includes all human beings on earth.

Penner—Self-consciousness of what?

Smith—Everything. Ourselves in relation to everything.

Penner—That's nothing. I don't have a self-consciousness of everything . . . . Wilfred Cantwell Smith is after what I would call the performance of certain kinds of things, which is indeed individual, and I'm over on the other side talking about how is it possible the individual has this competence to perform this? The two of us, as example the analogy, would be between linguistics and psycho-linguistics, the analogy would fit very nicely. Here it wouldn't be a matter that we disagree, but that we are . . . focusing on two sets of problems within a total kind of problem that we have, one coming in this way, one coming at it from the other way. But I think there's more to the disagreement that we have. It's not just that, because your [Smith's] intention is to understand persons, and I just don't know how that's possible unless we're back again into the problem of language games . . . that are presented to us because that's the avenue through which we do indeed understand.

      And if it is just personal, then in the end that's the side of skepticism I talked about in my paper. I think you're [Smith] a skeptic about the whole enterprise and it's not going to happen as far as you're concerned because we have to go to persons for this, and I find that in the end there are just too many persons that I'm going to have to go around trying to understand. That's impossible for me. So I'm doomed to failure. And I will have to take your introspections on understanding and so forth, and I find that, in the end, subjective and irrational.

Smith—. . . I think all we do is disagree there. I don't plead guilty to either subjectivism or irrationality. I simply claim that I have a different view of what it means to know and what the subject matter of our study really is.

Question (Directed to Prof. Smith)—I assume when you said that meaning is located in persons, . . . you think, you believe, you're making an important point . . . . Although you cannot verify this point by scientific means, could you, for clarification, specify its opposite or its converse? . . . At what point would you have to say, I was wrong.

Smith—Let's take the *upanayana* ceremony. I take it that Prof. Penner feels that that ceremony has a specific meaning. Now I claim that the ceremony as such has no meaning at all. The meaning is in the minds and heart and lives of certain Hindus who perform it or observe it.

      An example of evidence in favor of this is the fact that to Muslims it doesn't mean a thing. Or if it means anything it means superstition, stupidity, oppression, various other things . . . . To some other people in Japan it doesn't mean anything . . . . So I don't think the meaning lies in the structure but in the minds and hearts of the people, and it varies from day to day, century to century; not radically . . . but it isn't constant. I would guess that for a very sensitive imaginative certain type of boy it is more meaningful than it was for his brother. And less meaningful than it was for his father before him. This is the kind of thing I mean.

Now this would be shown to be false, if it could be demonstrated to me that the actual procedure as such, apart from who does it, has meaning. But I don't think it has any meaning whatever, in itself. Like the word *Om*.

Neusner—Could I say something about this? You [Smith] had one sentence that says it has no meaning, and the next sentence is, it means a great deal to the boy or the father. And I'm not clear as to what is being denied in the light of what you're willing to say. I will now beg the question one step further. You say to the Muslim it has no meaning. The next sentence is, "It's disgusting." So it has a meaning.

Smith—I say it *may* be disgusting.

Neusner—For the purposes of discussion, . . . that to me is a statement of weight and significance, just as much as if you said it means all the things Prof. Penner said it meant. I'm not clear as to what you're denying anymore. Are you saying, as you would say of a picture, the artist says the picture speaks for itself? . . .

So we have the problem, beyond a particular ritual, of what we think one can say about it, of what makes sense of it. I think it's a meaning to say, "it makes no sense at all," or "this speaks to my passage from childhood to the ascetic life," and so forth. I grant you . . . that a wide variety of possible meanings may be adduced. The one thing I don't follow is what you're denying in the sentence which precedes your meaning statement. Now you'll forgive me, I'm not a philosopher, . . . but I would like a clearer notion of what I'm supposed to deny or what you want to deny. I'm disposed to deny that there's an infinity of meanings . . . .

If we talked about a table, or the sun: you said the sun only has meaning according to what it means to me or to you . . . . Is it hard to agree that there is a very large corpus of words that we use in common meaning pretty much the same thing? . . .

Penner—. . . I think the personal position of meaning has consequences for me that I really worry about, politically, economically, all kinds of places, because . . . if it is the case that meaning inheres in a person, so that the meaning of the *upanayana* ritual is inherent in the human being that expresses it, or acts it out, and that it is meaningless to the Muslim, that is analogous to saying that Japanese, or English, or Chinese, that is the speaking of it, is meaningful only to the speakers of that language and meaningless when it is uttered to someone who only understands English. Now to a certain extent that's true. When someone starts uttering Japanese to me, I'm sure, since I don't understand Japanese, it's meaningless. But that does not imply . . . that the meaning of . . . any language . . . inheres in the minds, or the heart, of the person who's speaking it.

Smith—I claim that the meaning of Japanese resides in the Japanese-speaking community, and that if they all died, and it became impossible for anyone else ever to learn Japanese, then the meaning of that would evaporate.

Penner—But the instances of meaning in Japanese are instances of language. That's all I'm trying to get hold of . . . .

Smith—But if all human beings were obliterated, and you were left only with crocodiles, or stones, then meaning would also have disappeared. Meaning is a human affair.

Baird—How would one explain the meaning of something like the Rosetta Stone, in which the availability of one language enables you to decipher the other, even though there aren't living people who can tell you this is the case?

Smith—As I said, if the Japanese people disappear, even so they would leave behind them ways in which the rest of us, if we were smart enough, could recover the language, and indeed we did with the Rosetta Stone. During the interval . . . from 500 A.D. to 1800, I don't think the Rosetta Stone meant anything . . . and since that time it has again become meaningful . . . .

There are so many words on which we all agree that it is perfectly reasonable to make a short cut and say that the word "table" means this . . . . It would be very cumbersome to go through the long process of saying that there are a lot of people for whom the word "table" means this . . . . But the word "table" doesn't inherently mean this. Children grow up with the feeling, in our country, that the French are funny people—they call *fenêtre* what is *really* a window.

Question—You can certainly point out that to two different individuals the word "cross" might refer to the same physical object, but if one is a Christian, and one is a Hindu, that doesn't exhaust the meaning that's involved, even though the word is the same and we understand the same physical object to be the point of reference.

Penner—Therefore, the meaning of "cross" is not a personal decision.

Smith—"Cross" is a good example, because surely to many Jews the cross is a symbol of oppression, persecution and meanness. To many Christians it's a symbol of salvation, redemption, suffering, love, and so on. I would claim that there is nothing, but nothing, in a cross that signifies either redemption or persecution; but human history being what it is, human beings have reacted in certain ways, have done the things they've done in such a way that this particular symbol . . . has become, for Christians, symbolic of this, and perhaps for someone else . . . .

Neusner—But these are not private decisions.

Smith—Of course not.

Neusner—These are cultural, and social, . . .

Smith—Maybe the difficulty lies here. When I say personal I don't mean individual. The opposite of personal is not social. Society is personal. The opposite of personal is impersonal. The opposite of individual is society. Of course I'm talking primarily about societies in the *upanayana* ceremony. The meaning of it is lodged in the Hindu community. By personal I certainly don't mean individual. That's why I say my ultimate interest is in corporate self-consciousness of the entire human race, where we can transcend the limits of our separate societies and join the total society, but we'll never get beyond that. And as I see it the scientist, the scientifically-oriented student of human affairs, the behavioral scientist in particular, has as a kind of model of his knowledge of human affairs that sort of objectivity which human beings have vis-a-vis the physical world, because they are all outside it, and they look *at* it. But in the *human* world we are *inside*, and to hope to arrive at a point where our knowledge of human affairs is that of an outsider looking on, seems to me destructive of the very thing we most want to arrive at.

Penner—First of all, structuralism does not stand outside the structure. Someone said it's not a thing, inside or outside.

The second thing is, Prof. Smith, when you say we will never get beyond it, that's the skeptic position: we will never get beyond a certain question.

Now I just can't say that . . . . It's not a matter if I want to or not; it's just that my reflections about questions and so forth always lead me to thinking, maybe we can . . . .

Smith—This is marvelous, because you feel that it would be an advance if we could arrive at that external view for the whole human race. I take back that we'll never get beyond it. I'd rather think it may be possible to look at the human race impersonally. And I think scientists who look at human affairs that way are disproving my point that it can't be done. It can be done, and it strikes me as disastrous.

You [Prof. Penner] are so wedded to the scientific thing that you feel that if only we can incorporate the history of religions into the scientific enterprise, then we will have arrived.

Penner—You say it's a disaster. I want to know what the implications of that one are . . . . Where is the disaster?

Neusner—Let me try to cut the knot here.

Through your [Smith's] two papers you kept [focusing upon] . . . what you are really against. It came out a moment ago—the opposite of personal is impersonal. That brings together the entire argument of the first paper against methodology, and I can now think of instances [in] which this was what was not stated, but clearly implied. And again, the insistence in the second paper [upon recognizing] no one meaning in the text and so forth, not because of the historical problems, but because of the limitation imposed by the assertion that there is indeed a meaning at some one point . . . which governs the later development.

But I'm not sure if I have correctly interpreted what is meant, that you have directed your criticism in the right place, or that it's germane to the issue of methodology.

It's one thing to say, I'm angry with the impersonality of modern life, specifically produced by science, . . . the de-personalization of the individual would be high on the agenda.

That's one thing to say and I think that most people in point of fact would agree with you. But it's another thing to trace that negative phenomena back to particular modes of inquiry without taking those intermediate steps, that I haven't seen taken . . . . I would be interested to see how I get from the rejection of the impersonality of

modern science and scholarship . . . with the steps of that point, to the
critique of methodology. It is true that you could point, quite correctly,
to gross examples of an utter disinterest in persons on the part of people
who are social scientists. I felt at that time that you had been somewhat
unfair to the social sciences and the reason I felt it was unfair is that I
make the same complaints to my friends in sociology and they tell me,
"It's bad sociology, you're right."

So I'd like to pursue, if we can, the logic that leads from the
rejection of the impersonality of the modern world to the rejection of
methodology in a concern for the abstract articulation of how we do
our work in favor of . . . doing the work. That, I think, I can link to
your problem with the text . . . .

Smith—I am not in any fashion against science. I am against the
application of what looks to be scientific method—natural-science
method—to human affairs . . . to the study, the understanding of human
affairs. The application of what seems to be the natural-science
method, in the study of human affairs, insofar as it is impersonalism, . . .
is intellectually calculated to miss what it's attempting to understand,
because I think, on theoretical grounds, that you cannot understand
persons if you don't recognize that they're persons.

Comment (From the floor)—It would seem that the nub of the question
is, that with reference to any specific religious act, Prof. Smith
would say that how we find out the influence, the impact, the meaning
of that act, is to ask the people who do it.

But with regard to Prof. Penner, what he did with the *upanayana*
rite he could do without any reference to the people who actually do
it, and he could take that structure and become convinced that indeed
that is the structure of the rite, no matter what the people who actually
do it said, just as he implied you can understand the syntax of the
language even though the people who actually speak the language are
totally ignorant of it, and it seems that the difference between the two
of you is what you conceive the discipline to be able to do. You
[Prof. Smith] would say that one goes to the people and finds out what
they think, what they believe, what they understand themselves to be
doing, and Prof. Penner says, you can get to the inherent structures,
which are somehow inherent in the very act itself, even though people
may not realize that that structure is there.

Neusner—That's a very good point.

Smith—Very nice.

I learned last night most of what I know about the *upanayana*
ceremony, except in a very vague, distant way. I knew it took place, I
never heard it described . . . . And I came away from it with a better
understanding. I felt I understood things about it a lot better, for
which I was grateful.

I also came away feeling that all that I had learned had come not
from the structuralists' input into that presentation, but from what
Prof. Penner had learned from Sanskrit sources and the like and had
surreptitiously brought in, put up the diagram. He put words: north,

south, east, west. How did he know that north symbolizes man, dawn, etc.? Because he had read it in Sanskrit texts. Nothing structuralist there. And that south meant whatever it meant, and so on. Then even the fact that for them north, south, east, west, he said, "mediate"—an enormously connotative word, that! Mediation between east and west: that wasn't in the diagram. It was in his words.

A point . . . which struck me quite vividly in reading it, was that apparently the high point of the ceremony is when first the *acarya* recites and the boy repeats the Gayatri mantra, which, if I get it right, says, "O Savitri, greatest and fairest god, brilliant . . . grant me knowledge." Now it occurred to me that part of the meaning of this ceremony—and I guess, from talking to such *brahmans* as I have among my friends, that this is a very important part indeed—is that the ceremony consecrates, heightens, the boy's sense of knowledge; it gives him a feeling that it is extremely important. He may rattle the words off; or he may take them very seriously: it is a personal matter. But the meaning would come partly from this mantra; partly from the fact that for 2-3 weeks, 2-3 months before that, there would be mounting tension in the household . . . . That occurs in all our homes when a religious festival is in the offing. If he's sensitive (if he's not, of course, it's mechanical), if he's very sensitive, this fact . . . of his household's attitude to the sacred thread ceremony . . . would affect the meaning for him. Then at the very height of it this "knowledge" bit comes, and I would guess that out of this he may well get (though he may well not; this depends on him, and not merely on the ceremony itself) the same kind of thing that Prof. Neusner told us about with the rabbis—a feeling that knowledge, the pursuit of knowledge, is sacred, is terribly important, is worthwhile by itself. For him, the meaning of the ceremony may be the absolute importance of knowing.

I don't think a person who didn't know Sanskrit, who hadn't been to India . . . however good a structuralist he might be, could have done that presentation.

Penner—I confess I was using surface structure terms. I said this was a crude model because one of the postulates of structuralism is that you cannot explicate the structure by the surface units, and I was doing that.

It's just a matter of going from that . . . to show you one more diagram. Unfortunately, . . . it's terribly impersonal because it's a matter of logical formula which would show that formula that deep structure will generate, that structure in the system.

. . . I don't want to deny speech acts, or ritual performances; this becomes another issue. To utter a sentence, to perform the speaking of the English language, that's one thing. We can study that. But there's also what's called the competency, the ability to do that. These are two foci. Obviously we wouldn't be sitting here talking about religion or the history of religion if there weren't persons who acted that way or who spoke that way, and so forth. So it's not to deny this, it's just to say that in order to perform a speech act, I have to be able to explicate, as an historian of religions, how it's possible you can do that. And that then shoves me back to what you would want to call the impersonal, what I would want to call a deep structure, which allows me to do that.

Neusner—That last claim, Prof. Penner, that . . . you would show a logic which would always produce the same thing: I must tell you I think that would be a very neat trick, and I would be very happy to see it because I think this is what I am after . . . . My inclination is that this is so. And we should be able to do it and that there should be a larger system . . . which is going to unify the whole, and while preserving its distinctiveness, also reveal logic. I would be very happy to see that.

Penner—In your paper, Prof. Neusner, you did say something about the intellectual life had to be accountable to the sacred, or that the rite is the intellectual conversation . . . in Judaism they don't have *upanayana* ceremonies. Obviously, . . . but when you come along as an historian of Judaism and tell me, look, that's not where you look for rituals in Rabbinic Judaism, here's where you look for it, I see if that structure can come into that one.

Neusner—If that came to a deeper structure for our system, which I think would be exceedingly difficult, both to discover and then to convey, if you find it and show how it works, and not convey it to those of us not familiar with the language, it will be a very tragic failure.

Smith—But if this were found, surely the similarity (and this Savitri mantra opened up a similarity between Jews and Hindus on the sacredness of knowing), if there were found a similarity between Jewish ritual and reasoning, and Hindu . . . the similarity, I would claim, would not lie in the structure of these rituals but in the structure of human personality; that human beings are that type of creature for whom knowing, the use of the mind, is able to be sacralized, perceived as sacred. Then there are a number of symbolic forms that human beings have dreamed up across the centuries through which they have symbolized such things. But the nub of the issue doesn't lie in the nature of those symbolic forms. It lies in the nature of the human personality; and in the nature of knowing, if you like. I personally also agree with intellectualism . . . that's why I'm not irrational. I believe that the use of the mind is in fact holy . . . . But *that* is where the similarity lies, not in the conformability of the symbolic forms. After all, the Jewish thing is aniconic; and iconoclasm is a very profound . . . .

Question (Directed to Prof. Penner)—What do you see as the difference between structuralism and essentialism?

Penner—I would take essentialism to be—I'm looking for the essence of something in the world . . . . Phenomenology and philosophical phenomenologies also are looking for the essences of things. And, this is usually based on intuition . . . . In the end what I usually get is a description of someone's intuition about the essences of things. I not only get the intuitions of the essences but I get disagreement as to what the intuitions of the essences are. This goes on and on and on and people debate about their intuitions, which ones I'm going to take as the valid ones.

And structuralism, as I understand it, in all of its forms, and there are lots of disagreements within that particular postulate, would deny essentialism. At least that's what they state. And again I think a good book to capture this would be Piaget's *Structuralism*.

Goldstein[3]—Every theologian I have read claims to be a middle-of-the-road man. May I make a plea for the middle-of-the-road.

I am not interested in one method that will cover all areas at all times.

The history of academic research shows us that there are many good methods that have their limitations because of what they are designed to do.

Can we not agree on a more moderate position?

Smith—That [is] what I thought I was saying.

Question—. . . I cannot help but feel that this method [structuralism] too, will turn out very strong limitations, which says nothing against it if it is used in the appropriate manner.

Smith—Certainly I have no objection to anybody being a structuralist if he wants to. What I object to is the insistence that we should all be structuralists, or that it matters. If anyone who is a structuralist . . . does good work, I will applaud. And if I do good work the fact that I am not a structuralist (or if it turns out that maybe I am; I don't care) that's fine too. I simply want to do good work.

I also want to find out what it's like to be a human being, which it seems to me for the history of religions is one of the most crucial keys to discover.

VII

POSTSCRIPT: METHODOLOGY, THEORY AND EXPLANATION IN THE STUDY OF RELIGION

Robert D. Baird

It is reasonably clear that in this symposium the two poles are found in Prof. Smith, who has grave misgivings with the drift of academia into disciplines and the ensuing emphasis on method, and Prof. Penner, who seems to embody what Prof. Smith most fears—an attempt to construct a grand theory of religion which will finally enable us to explain the phenomena.

Some attention to the presentations and discussions also suggests that the terms method, methodology, explanation, and theory are used in more than one way by the participants. This is not surprising. Moreover, unless one values a monolithic use of language (which is not likely to take place even if it were desired), varied usage does not hinder communication provided it does not hide the fact that the meanings are not uniform. It is helpful, however, in discussing such matters, to clarify the meanings of terms so that we can know just what is being discussed and where the participants do indeed differ.

I have argued that clarity in the academic study of religion requires clarity in the meaning of the categories used, and that since most words are lexically ambiguous (have more than one meaning), they must be rendered unambiguous through the use of functional or stipulative definitions.[1] I did not argue that definitional clarity would eliminate all divergencies or answer all questions, but I did contend that such definitional clarity was a prerequisite to understanding the issues and identifying potential answers. This is true for the historian of religions in his definition of the primary categories of religion and history. Such clarification of terminology would also help to place in perspective some of the differences between Professors Penner and Smith. I might wish that it would dissolve all of their differences, so that I could agree with both of them and they could agree with each other, but functional definitions cannot be expected to resolve substantive matters.

It is my intention, then, to offer functional definitions of method, methodology, theory, and explanation with the hope of being able to indicate the bounds of each. It is further my intention to examine *some* of the proposals of Professors Penner and Smith in the light of these distinctions. I will then consider where Prof. Neusner fits into this scheme.

To begin with, *method* in the study of religions is the procedure or procedures used to acquire, organize, and analyze materials which are considered religious. This analysis involves the formulation of questions for which one is seeking answers. These questions may be: What is the deep structure of religion? or, What is the faith of these persons? The procedures required in either case would be the method employed.

Methodology does not refer to the procedure employed, but to an analysis of the assumptions and logical limitations of the method. Hence, methodology is the logic of method. Every student of religion has a method, however inadequate or inconsistent it might be. One cannot study anything systematically without using some procedure or other. However, not all scholars have attended to methodology, that is, to the analysis of the logic of their method, its limits, and how it relates or does not relate to other methods. Some scholars simply stumble through their material without caring to articulate exactly what they are doing. Some stumble more skillfully than others. Choosing not to discuss methodology simply leaves the logic of one's procedure to chance. It means that one simply chooses not to analyze in a logical manner what questions he is asking of his material and chooses not to determine the limitations of such questions. That does not mean that the work is rendered illogical. Some scholars do stumble rather well. But unless someone analyzes the logic of a given procedure, we will simply not know whether the conclusions represent valid knowledge or not. Of course, if a community of "scholars" simply agree by common consent to stumble along together, there is little one can do about it.

Theory of religion refers not to an analysis of the method or procedure being used, but to an analysis of *the thing* that is found through the use of a given method and is deemed to be religion. Theory of religion is not to be confused with methodology. The former presupposes the latter. It is only after we have clarified our terms through the use of functional definitions and have determined the questions we are interested in asking of our data that we are in a position to analyze the "thing."[2] But to theorize about religion is not to theorize about the word, but to theorize about the thing to which the word has been determined to point.

What, then, about the word *explanation*? Explanation has taken place when one has produced a true theory about the nature of the thing. Method alone will not explain religion. However, theories do—at least when they are true theories. Theories of religion are inevitably normative, for they are concerned with offering explanations of a dimension of reality. They are not concerned merely with defining the meanings of words, but with giving an explanation of the things to which the words point. When might one be said to have explained religion?— when one has shown *why* there is rather than is not such a thing at all. This involves one directly in metaphysics and theory. And a concrete rite or belief may be said to have been explained when it has been shown *why* it exists where it does rather than somewhere else.

It should be apparent that there are certain implications which derive from this set of definitions. First, although methodology can be avoided (one can perhaps practice his craft and stay employed without it), the logic of method is a necessary part of validating the knowledge that one purports to acquire through any given procedure or method.

Second, methodology and theory are not the same. Theory always deals with the thing while methodology may not. One may, for example, set out a reasoned method on the basis of a series of functional definitions so that the method being analyzed is heuristic in intent. This means it is only dealing with relationships—this being the case, that follows. This can be done on the descriptive level, may have no interest in explaining *why* there is religion, and may settle for an analysis of *how* religion appears or functions. Since it is only interested in studying the multitudinous forms of religion in terms of the functional definition given, it does not involve one in a theory of religion. To theorize about religion would be a further step in which one then proposes to *explain why* persons have ultimate concerns at all, or *why* archaic man seeks to live in the sacred as much as possible. One may take this further step, but it is hardly inevitable.

Third, and closely related, is that the history of religions so defined does not seek in the end to explain religion, but merely to understand. Understanding takes place on a variety of levels, one of which is explanation on the basis of theory. It may well be better not to speak of historical explanation as much as historical understanding. The reason for this is that it is not possible within the limits of historical knowledge to explain *why* the *upanayana* rite is practiced by a certain Indian and not by a certain Japanese. That is, it is not possible to show *why* it *has* to be where it is in fact found rather than somewhere else. Explanation suggests necessity. Hence it is best related to a true theory of religion. Of course, if the theory is false then religion has not been explained, even if the proposed theory is of explanatory intention. On the other hand, one might well understand religion on a variety of levels short of explanation when one gains a knowledge of the *how* of religion.

How, then, do these categories assist us in understanding the divergencies that appear to exist between Professors Penner, Smith, and Neusner? Prof. Penner's presentations indicate that the distinctions which I have made between methodology and theory, understanding and explanation are not followed. "Since understanding and explaining religion is our central concern . . ."—so begins Penner's discussion of the *upanayana* rite.[3] Several pages later, it is clear that the two terms are used interchangeably when he speaks of "understanding or explaining religion."[4]

Functionalism, then, does not enable us to understand religion because it does not explain religion. It does not explain religion because its theory is inadequate. Hence functionalism fails to answer the *why* question, and so does not give us the *meaning* of religion. It is this meaning of religion, derived from an adequate theory of religion, which answers the why question which is the object of Penner's search.

> The question that immediately comes to mind is, "What is this kind of language and behavior all about? What does it *mean*?" The first thing that comes to mind is the answer that this is the way Hindus teach their children their religious and moral tradition. Now, this is certainly true. But things become a little more difficult when we ask *why* Hindu boys learn about their tradition in this kind of way. *Why* does he have to perform this ritual before he can go on to learn the Vedas? *Why* is it the case that if he doesn't perform the ritual he will not be able to perform others? *Why* does he have to go through the rites of purification . . .[5]

The meaning of the ritual will not have been found until the *why* question has been answered. Functionalism's failure to answer that question points to its inadequacy.

> This means that functionalism will not be able to explain
> *why* the *upanayana* ritual, or the use of mantras, or poly-
> theism appeared in Hinduism and not, for example,
> in Islam.[6]

Penner explicitly states that it is the theory which explains
religion. Such an assertion would fit the functional definitions offered
at the beginning of this "postscript."

> If we assume that at some point we can state the theory we
> are using to explain religion it becomes obvious that such an
> explanation will be in the context of a theory about
> beliefs, concerns, values, and the like. That is to say, it is
> our theory about concerns and beliefs that explains
> religion . . . .[7]

The problem of meaning is the crucial problem for historians of
religions,[8] and at the same time the problem which they have ignored.[9]
The history of religions does not need unique theories to explain
religion. Since meaning is a semantic problem, and since it is the
meaning of religion for which we are searching, the solution is to be
found in semantic theory. Just as linguists have sought for the "deep
structure" of a language, so the historian of religions should get on the
trail of the "deep structure" of religion. And, however one chooses to
state the relationship between meaning and "deep structure," it can be
said that when one has found the "deep structure" one has located the
meaning of religion as well. Then one could also say that one has
explained religion in a manner that functionalism and essentialism have
failed to do.

In rejecting theory, Professor Smith thereby rejects this search for
meaning. For Penner this search for meaning is not sinful, but important
and inevitable. On the other hand, Penner sees Smith as being involved
in a theory of persons—however theoretically indisposed he pretends
to be.

For Penner, the search for the meaning of religion cannot be
completed by dealing with persons, nor through the summary or
accumulation of a given religious tradition.[10] But through the use of
modern semantic theory the historian of religions will be able to come
up with a valid explanation of religion through a discovery of the
"deep structure" of religion.

Utilizing my functional definitions, Professor Smith is correct in
holding that it is not necessary to do theory. Penner seems to have
suggested correctly that Smith's concern with persons is more than
heuristic. Smith's concern with persons is theoretical, and it is this

which enables him to say that to treat persons as less than persons (in his sense) or as adjuncts to economic or social theorizing is sinful. It is sinful in his system since a theory of religion is posited which makes persons (as he understands them) central to the understanding. One could define religion functionally as the study of persons and thereby do away with the theoretical dimension, but Smith does not. Hence his commitment is not merely methodological, but theoretical as well.

Penner seems to be at the beginning of a quest for "deep structure." But as far as his papers go, he leaves us somewhat uninformed about the "deep structure" and how it differs from or is distinguishable from the "surface structure." In his first paper he proposed that he was going to engage in a structural analysis of the *upanayana* rite, but when it was finished he conceded that all he had offered was a "surface structure." He had not offered an answer to the *why* question and hence he stopped short of offering an *explanation* of that rite. This is not to say that it cannot be done. But it is to say that it has not yet been shown what *is* involved or how it is to be accomplished. Perhaps we will not know if it can be done until it is actually tried—which adds some weight to Smith's concern over methodologists and theorists. Methodologists sometimes appear to be like meat-cutters who sharpen their knives away without actually cutting any meat.

Penner's reluctance to begin his procedures with a definition of religion is what requires that he see theory as unavoidable. It also lands him squarely within the essentialist camp, quite apart from his protests to the contrary. He recognizes that various definitions of "religion" have been offered.[11] Yet even though he wants to work toward a theory of religion he seems to think that we generally know what we mean by the word. By not giving adequate attention to the distinction between words and the things to which they point the argument is less than clear. The following statement is made at the beginning of his first paper.

> To say, for example, that religion is "ultimate concern" implies that an explanation of religion, assuming the definition is formally adequate, will be embedded in a theory regarding concerns. To assert that religion is a "belief system" implies an explanation of religion within some theory about beliefs.
>
> If we assume that at some point we can state the theory we are using to explain religion it becomes obvious that such an explanation will be in the context of a theory about beliefs, concerns, values, and the like. That is to say, it is our theory about concerns and beliefs that explains religion; religion is a feature of concerns or beliefs.[12]

Here Penner begins with an assertion about the nature of definitions of religion and the relationship of such definitions to theories of religion. When we move to the second paragraph (in the above quotation), where he speaks of using a theory to explain religion, he is clearly referring to the thing. This is correct: theories explain things. But in addition to the thing religion is the word "religion" which we use when referring to the thing. I earlier argued that it would be better if we limited our use of the lexically ambiguous word "definition" to words rather than things.[13] If Penner is saying, in above paragraph one, that to define "religion" functionally (pledge that one will use the word in a given way) as "ultimate concern" is to involve one in a theory of ultimate concern, he is in error. Such definitions merely clarify *word* usage.

If, on the other hand, in the first paragraph (of the above quotation) Penner is referring to the thing religion, and contrary to my point, is seeking to define the thing as ultimate concern, then he is correct that such an explanation of the thing involves a theory of ultimate concern. A definition is not simply a definition! If one is defining the nature or essence of the thing (assuming it is only one thing to which the word refers), then theory is certainly involved. If one is merely clarifying the usage of a word, no theory is required. (Now this may have implications for a theory of language, but does not involve one necessarily in a theory of religion.) To define a word simply means that when one uses it he means thus and so. One is not giving any theory about the nature of that thus and so. To insist that it is necessary to begin by defining the word "religion" is to recognize that the word has had several usages and clarification is necessary. But not to proceed by defining the word is to assume that the use of the word will be sufficient for all persons to intuit the same thing. And this is essentialism.[14] Hence Penner loses either way. If he sees the definition referred to in paragraph one as verbal, it does not require a theory. If he sees it as the definition of a thing he falls in with the essentialists whom he criticizes.

This failure to distinguish clearly between the word "religion" with its varied usages and the thing religion to which the word points in any given usage makes Penner's discussion of the problem of meaning somewhat obscure. Four statements from his discussion will be useful here.

> What we fail to realize, however, is that when we say "religion points to the sacred," or that the object of

religion is this or that, we are not making simple statements of fact. The question, "What is the meaning of religion?" or, "What is the reference of religion?" is not equivalent to "Where is the University of Iowa?"[15]

The point of this characterization is that when we do face the problem of semantics we usually solve it by equating meaning with reference. The fact that this shift is not a simple matter of fact can be seen in the complex debates which have gone on with regard to the adequacy of the reduction of meaning to reference.[16]

The pervasiveness of this theory in the study of religion will become evident when we remember that long ago it was simply assumed that the referent of religion was nature itself.[17]

It was not prolonged reflection on the adequacy of a theory of reference that shook us out of this magnificent explanation of religion.[18]

Now this discussion about meaning and the theory of reference does not clarify whether one is talking about the word "religion" or the thing to which it points. Whether this confusion is in the literature upon which Penner depends or merely in his utilization of it is of little consequence for our point.

To begin with, it seems obvious enough that our words do refer to something which stands beyond them—that to which they refer (at least many of them do). The word "religion" is not the same as the thing religion. We do use words (among them the word "religion") to refer to things. But the word and the thing are not identical even though the word should, if clearly used, enable us to bring the thing to mind.

The problem of meaning, however, appears to exist on another level. The problem of the meaning of religion involves one in an explanation of religion (quote 4, above) and that in turn implies a theory of religion (quote 3, above). But, when one states that religion refers to ultimate concern or that "religion points to the sacred," one is not necessarily involved in a theory about the meaning of the thing religion. The language may merely be intended to indicate how the word "religion" is to be used in a given context. Again, all definitions of religion are not involved in a *theory* of reference in the sense here discussed, but merely are indicating what thing it is to which the word refers. Meaning in the sense proposed by Penner has to do with the thing. What that thing is to which the word points can only be clarified by a functional or stipulative definition of the word.

I have argued that it is helpful for purposes of discussion to distinguish method from methodology, and methodology from theory and explanation. Penner does not do this. For him methodology and explanation and theory run together. For Penner, when one defines terms one is implying a theory about religion and hence also an explanation.

It is this tendency to run methodology and theory together that contributes to Prof. Smith's opposition to methodology. In terms of my definitions, Prof. Smith is not opposed to method and does not always take a hard line on methodology. He can be found both devaluing and affirming methodology.

> ... I feel that methodology is the massive red herring of modern scholarship, the most significant obstacle to intellectual progress, the chief distraction from rational understanding of the world.[19]

> When I affirm that the emphasis on method in modern university thinking disturbs or alienates me, I have to admit to myself that I too in some sense prize method, *and stress it*, and give loyalty to it; and I expect my students to do so.[20]

Smith is more concerned with a knowledge of things (in this case persons) than he is with method. As he sees it, the preoccupation with method has distracted scholars from a traditional humanistic concern with the real world. Instead they have concerned themselves with procedures and theories. He recognizes, however, that what some call methodology he calls the presuppositions or the conceptual framework of one's study. What Smith seems unwilling to abandon completely is either method (in terms of procedures—for example the examination of 25,000 book titles) or methodology which shows the limitations of any given method (even though a concentration on the latter appears distasteful to him). What he most of all shuns is a focus on theory which is more a history of recent Western thought. An emphasis on theory is more akin to philosophy of religion. For all of his misgivings, Smith is unable to shed completely his interest in methodology. But since method and theory are commonly aligned and not often distinguished, his rejection of a preoccupation with theory leads him also to reject a preoccupation with method or methodology. Now it is true that a *preoccupation* with method and methodology can also become a hindrance to ever examining the real world. But one can never examine the real world with any precision without method, even though one can do history without theory.

When Smith states that method should be fundamentally dispensable, he overstates his case.[21] Method, as a means of approaching the real world, is never dispensable without dispensing with knowledge as well. It is true that method alone will only give us knowledge of method and not knowledge of the real world. But method is the means used for acquiring a knowledge of the real world and when it is dispensed with (either during or at the end of the investigation) knowledge is also forfeited. Whether the analysis of 25,000 book titles is a valid way of arriving at "religious insight" is a matter that methodology (the logic of the method) will decide. And it will also decide if that procedure is worth pursuing in other concrete cases.

Prof. Smith is making a true statement when he says:

> I think that it can be shown that any given method to some degree predetermines the results that will be got by using it. It is also the case that any given set of preconceptions to some extent predetermines the results also.[22]

Smith's following argument, however, does not point out how *every* scholar is bound by his questions, and at the same time equally capable of asking a different set of questions should he become dissatisfied with his previous ones. Smith goes on to argue that it is imperative that one's presuppositions be modifiable in the process of one's investigations. It is his contention that humane students of religion are more ready to modify their presuppositions than methodological students are to modify their methodologies. If this is indeed the case, the fault is not with methodology. A scholar who has articulated a methodology is as capable (leaving aside personal qualities or the lack of them) of modifying his preconceptions as is the humane scholar. If, for example, he is looking for the structure of religion (even the "deep structure" if it can be shown to exist), and if there is a means for falsifying the structure proposed to have been found, then it seems the structuralist would be most willing to continue the search for another structure. Penner ends his presentation with the following:

> What if it is the case that a well-formed theory of semantics cannot be constructed? What then? Well, for one thing we will have learned a great deal. We will have learned, for example, that chunks of history, as chunks of sound patterns, will not serve as a substitute for our failure . . . .[23]

It is true that although he may, after repeated failures try another method, if the structuralist fails to find the deep structure by reason of a finding being falsified, he will probably continue to look for that deep structure. Modification takes place within methodologically defined limits. The only way to provide for further modification is to exchange one method for another—that is, if Penner were to reject structuralism and accept Smith's interest in persons. But is not the same true for Smith's humane personalism? The humane scholar is willing to modify his preconceptions in the light of evidence within the limits imposed by his method, that is, the questions he has chosen to ask or not to ask. If, therefore, his interest is in persons, what he finds out about thos persons in direct contact can modify his preconceptions about those persons. But is is not possible to discover through this interest in persons the deep structure of religion. If one's interest in persons remains, all modifications must take place within that interest or that limitation (for it is such), however valid it might be in itself. But to modify the presuppositions beyond that would require that one give up that interest in persons for an interest in structures or society, and that would be to exchange one method for another. Even if it were true that methodologists are less likely to modify their preconceptions than humane scholars, that is not a requirement due to the nature of methodology, but has to do with the qualities of the persons involved.

There does not seem to be any inherent reason why some anthropologist might not test his anthropological theory with a study of Lebanese villagers in whom he has no personal interest. He will never come to a personal understanding in that manner, but he does not desire to do so. Such a search may well be distasteful to Prof. Smith, but to protest too vigorously would be unbecoming a "methodological pluralist." Nor does the anthropologist's non-personal interests make him any less willing in principle to modify his preconceptions if he finds that his theory is falsified in the light of his findings. It does preclude him from a personal understanding of the villagers, but what *moral* argument could possible be offered that would require us to conclude with Smith that that is what he *must* be interested in? On the other hand, one whose interest is personal rather than theoretical may also modify his preconceptions about Lebanese villagers, but not his view that what is important is personal understanding. To do so would be to change that method for another.

Methodological deliberation demands that one articulate the questions one is asking, but it does not demand that all use the same method—whether personal or impersonal. And the results will have to be evaluated in the light of the question asked *and* the evidence adduced. That means that it would do no good for Penner to reject Smith's personalism because it did not lead to a verified deep structure of religion. Nor will it be acceptable for Smith to reject Penner's structuralism because it does not lead to a deeper understanding of persons in the concrete and particular.

Whether a methodological pluralist, or one who follows one method, Smith is proposing that one use certain approaches or methods.[24] And these, whether he likes it or not, have been developed within disciplinary contexts. To use the approaches of sociology, history, philology, psychology, and typology is to presuppose that one is familiar with them and that he knows their questions and limitations. This is the realm of methodology. Smith may be correct in suggesting that those who merely discuss methodology and theory get on with it and use their proposed methods to illuminate something. But how an emphasis on methodology can distort and disrupt knowledge is difficult to understand since all knowledge is acquired by some method. One may again question whether knowledge of the real world is furthered by persons who theorize without applying their methods or theories. But to claim that such concerns obstruct understanding while at the same time claiming not to be against method is not rational.

In seeking to return scholars to the study of the real world, and to move them from their apparent preoccupation with methodology and theory, Prof. Smith has stated his case in the extreme. When he double- and triple-checks his conclusions,[25] it is true that he is not double- and triple-checking the method. But he is checking the results by some method or other, and if the logic of the method is never checked, its legitimacy is subject to doubt and so are his conclusions—no matter how many times they are checked. If one says that the method is authenticated by the legitimacy of the results, the question is: How are the results legitimatized if not by that method or some other? Surely they are not self-authenticating. That would hardly qualify for a rational inquiry.

If Prof. Penner's case is extreme in holding that all methodology involves theory, Prof. Smith's case is extreme in holding that methodology is "the most significant obstacle to intellectual progress."

What, then, about Prof. Neusner? In terms of the functional definitions I have offered, he is not articulating a method, but following one. Nor is he discussing methodology or theories of religion. By beginning with a chosen definition of religion he avoids the essentialist dilemma. His attention to concrete particulars rather than abstract theory cannot help but appeal to Prof. Smith. And, although he is not searching for the "deep structure" of religion, because he does not openly condemn the search, he offers Prof. Penner little with which to disagree.

REJOINDER

Wilfred Cantwell Smith

The decision to publish the proceedings of this Conference has placed me in a moral dilemma. On the one hand, I feel that in general the quantity of academic publication in our day is excessive and that only those things should appear in print that their authors regard as thought through and polished, and with which they are fully satisfied as a final position that will probably stand up well and long to criticism. I also feel that in particular I myself have attained any adequacy that I may have managed to attain in my scholarly writing by, first of all, achieving some fairly satisfying understanding of positions other than my own before venturing to write about them and then in verification ascertaining that those concerned can recognize my interpretation of them as authentic. On both grounds, manifestly, my predilection would necessarily be to withhold my own part in these particular presentations until I have made much more progress. It is evident that I have yet much to learn, both in coming to grips with others' positions in a way that both they and I can agree on as an acceptable portrayal, and in making intelligible to others my own perceptions and judgments. Specifically, it seems evident that I have neither fully appreciated Prof. Penner's position nor enabled him to see what I was getting at.

On the other hand, our symposium was too small and too integrated for one contributor unilaterally to abstain. It would be discourteous to our very hospitable hosts and to my more accomplished colleagues if I were to push my own procrastinations, however well founded.

In the end, this latter consideration carried the day. The unperfectedness of my own presentations was outweighed by the imperative to go along.

Disquieting, however, was the recognition that a compromise, even, was not feasible, in the form of revising what was here set forth—since this would disrupt the continuity and indeed the integrity of the "discussions." I am not wise enough to say on the spur of the moment and in the heat of debate what will fully satisfy even me, let alone others, over the long haul, nor unwise enough to have learned nothing from the Conference. On the former point: during the final panel, within a minute or two of certain statements I thought of serious modifications that it would then disrupt the ensuing discussion to go back and make, though I am restless at the statements' being given permanence in unmodified form now. On the latter: since we met in Iowa, I have mulled over the issues; have come to some clearer insight (I think: though I have not been able yet to test this carefully) into the theses of those (especially Prof. Penner) from whom, so far as I could understand them, I differed; and have moved a little toward a conspectus. This last, however, is a mighty matter, and will not readily be attained. It is also, however, an important matter, and a striving towards it should not readily be abandoned. (The conspectus towards which I find myself moving promises to be, appropriately enough, historical and comparative.)

On the whole, the Conference confirmed my discernment that in the general direction of the recent drift of the interpretive pre-suppositions of academic theorizing there is much that is unfortunate. It also deepened my awareness that to do anything constructive about this problem will be highly demanding. I do not feel that the contributions here presented adequately rise to those exacting demands.

Ideally I should be disposed to defer the corporate production until all concerned had transcended their divergences in a joint state-ment, at the least setting forth a mutually accepted clarification of differences.

Our unfailingly generous chairman, however, has been kind enough to make two concessions; and these being granted, I have in the end acquiesced. One is that my "seminar" on the interpretation of scripture be withdrawn, the ensuing discussion and the later typed-from-tape recording of the presentation itself having shown that the thesis (in which I still believe) was inadequately developed. The other is to allow me to enter this present disclaimer. I would have preferred to work further on these questions before publishing; and to persuade Prof. Penner to work further with me. This seems not feasible, however. In any case, it is perhaps not fully clear—even after the Conference—whether it is more important to wrestle the more valiantly, relent-lessly, with these issues, or to move ahead rather with the substantive task of solid studies of human religious life. (Prof. Neusner's two papers owed their excellence largely to the fact that they dealt with substantive rather than with procedural matters.) We in the West are perhaps more likely (than through any narcissistic focus) to become intelligently self-critical of our conceptual orientations the more we can manage to take with sufficient seriousness and realism our endeavor accurately and genuinely to understand those quite different orienta-tions of other ages and civilizations and groups that are our subject matter.

FOOTNOTES

CHAPTER I

1. This indicates a question from the floor where the identity of the questioner is uncertain (Ed.).
2. Robert P. Scharlemann, Professor of Religion, The University of Iowa.

CHAPTER II

1. Van A. Harvey, *The Historian and the Believer* (New York, 1966), pp. 258-59.
2. A. Leo Oppenheimer, *Ancient Mesopotamia* (Chicago, 1964), p. 30.
3. August Schlegel, quoted by Harvey, *op. cit.*, p. 4.
4. E.J. Bickerman, "Faux littéraires dans l'antiquité classique, en marge d'un livre récent," *Rivista di Filologia ē di Istruzione Classica* Vol. 101, 3rd series, 1973, 1, pp. 22-41, in particular, pp. 34-35.
5. Jacob Neusner, *The Idea of Purity in Ancient Judaism* (Leiden, 1973), with a critique by Mary Douglas; and Mary Douglas, *Purity and Danger* (London, 1966).
6. Jonathan A. Goldstein, Professor of Ancient History, The University of Iowa.
7. James F. McCue, Professor of Religion, The University of Iowa.

CHAPTER III

1. The synopsis of the ritual is based upon my own translation of the ritual. Relevant translations of the ritual can be found in the series, *Sacred Books of the East*, tr. by Max Müller; see *Shatapatha Brahmana*, and the various translations of the *Grihya Sutras*. J. Gonda provides useful bibliographies and descriptions of aspects of the ritual in his book *Change and Continuity in Indian Religion* (The Hague, 1965).
2. My colleague Edward Yonan and I have tried to clarify some of the misconceptions of the term "reduction" in, "Is a Science of Religion Possible?", *Journal of Religion*, 52 (1972), pp. 107-33.
3. The three explanatory models are taken from Carl G. Hempel, "The Logic of Functional Analysis," in *Readings in the Philosophy of the Social Sciences*, ed. by May Brodbeck (New York, 1968), pp. 191-95. The essay originally appeared in *Symposium on Sociological Theory*, ed. by Llewellyn Gross (New York, 1959).
4. For an excellent analysis of negative feedback systems, see Robert Brown, *Explanation in Social Science* (Chicago, 1963), Chapter IX.
5. See "What is Structuralism?", in W.G. Runciman, *Sociology in Its Place and Other Essays* (Cambridge, 1970), pp. 45-58. For an expansion and interpretation of the principles of structuralism, see Jean Piaget, *Structuralism* (New York, 1970).

CHAPTER V

1. I am indebted to Jerrold J. Katz for the framework of the last few paragraphs. His analysis of the situation in linguistics fits our own situation very nicely. For the complete critique, see Jerrold J. Katz, *Semantic Theory* (New York, 1972), Preface and Chapter I.
2. Stephen Ullmann, *Semantics* (Oxford, 1972), p. 54.
3. Wallace L. Chafe, *Meaning and the Structure of Language* (Chicago, 1970), p. 75.
4. Katz, *loc. cit.*, p. 2.
5. Willard V. Quine, *From a Logical Point of View* (Cambridge, Mass.), p. 47. Also quoted in Katz, p. 9.
6. Katz, *loc. cit.*, p. 3.
7. Ullmann, *Semantics*, p. 159. I am indebted to Ullmann for both the example of the "board" and the quote on Oliver Twist.
8. Katz, *loc. cit.*, p. 7.
9. Mary Douglas, "The Meaning of Myth," in *The Structural Study of Myth and Totemism*, ed. by Edmund Leach (London, 1967), pp. 49-69.
10. Claude Lévi-Strauss, *Totemism*, tr. by Rodney Needham (Boston, 1963), p. 69.
11. See J.J. Katz and J.A. Fodor, "The Structure of a Semantic Theory," *Language*, (1963), 39, pp. 170-210.
12. Katz, *loc. cit.*, pp. 4-6.
13. *Ibid.*, p. 7.
14. *Ibid.*, p. 21.

CHAPTER VI

1. Lecture, "Methodology and the Study of Religion: Some Misgivings."
2. "The Problem of Semantics in the Study of Religion."
3. Helen T. Goldstein, Assistant Professor of Religion, The University of Iowa.

CHAPTER VII

1. Robert D. Baird, *Category Formation and the History of Religions* (The Hague, 1971), especially chapter 1.
2. By "thing" I mean that to which the word points. It is not derogatory of persons in this context to call them "things."
3. Cf. p. 50.
4. Cf. p. 52.
5. *Ibid.* (emphasis added).
6. Cf. p. 56.
7. Cf. p. 79.
8. Cf. p. 80.
9. Cf. p. 81.
10. Cf. p. 84.

11. Cf. pp. 79, 80, 82.
12. Cf. p. 79.
13. *Category Formation and the History of Religions*, chapter 1.
14. *Ibid.*, p. 2.
15. Cf. p. 87.
16. Cf. p. 88.
17. *Ibid.*
18. *Ibid.*
19. Cf. p. 2.
20. Cf. p. 3.
21. Cf. p. 15.
22. Cf. p. 18.
23. Cf. p. 93.
24. Cf. p. 14.
25. Cf. p. 15.

CONTRIBUTORS

Wilfred Cantwell Smith is McCullough Professor of Religion and Chairman of the Department of Religion at Dalhousie University, Halifax, Nova Scotia. From 1964-1973 he was Professor of World Religions and Director of the Center for the Study of World Religions at Harvard University. He taught Islamic history at Forman Christian College at Lahore, and was Birks Professor of Comparative Religion at McGill University (1949-1963) where he founded and directed McGill's Institute of Islamic Studies.

Professor Smith has lived a fair part of his life in India and Pakistan, and has travelled widely throughout the Muslim world. He graduated in Oriental Languages from the University of Toronto (B.A., 1938) and from Princeton University (Ph.D., 1948).

He is the author of five books: *Modern Islam in India* (1943); *Islam in Modern History* (1957); *The Faith of Other Men* (1962); *The Meaning and End of Religion* (1963); and *Questions of Religious Truth* (1967).

Professor Smith is advisory editor for *The Muslim World*, the *Middle East Journal*, and *Religious Studies*.

Jacob Neusner is Professor of Religion at Brown University. He is the author of the following scholarly books: *A Life of Yohanan ben Zakkai* (awarded the Abraham Berliner Prize in Jewish History by Jewish Theological Seminary of America); *A History of the Jews in Babylon*, 5 vols. (1965-1970); *Development of a Legend: Studies on the Traditions Concerning Yohanan ben Zakkai* (1970); *Aphrahat and Judaism: The Christian-Jewish Argument in Fourth Century Iran* (1971); *The Rabbinic Traditions about the Pharisees before 70*, 3 vols. (1971). In addition he has edited a number of scholarly books and written and edited a number of textbooks.

Professor Neusner has held numerous fellowships, including a Guggenheim Memorial Foundation Fellowship, and is a past president of the American Academy of Religion (1968-1969).

Hans H. Penner is Phillips Professor of Religion at Dartmouth College. He is the author of several articles on methodology in the study of religion, including: "Poverty of Functionalism"; "Is Phenomenology a Method for the Study of Religion?"; "Is a Science of Religion Possible?"; and "Myth and Ritual: Wasteland or Forest of Symbols?"

Professor Penner received his Ph.D. in the history of religions at the University of Chicago, was the recipient of a Fulbright Award in 1965, and participated in the "Methodology Conference," University of Turku, Finland, in 1973.

Robert D. Baird is Professor of History of Religions at The University of Iowa, from which university he received his Ph.D. in 1964. He is the author of *Category Formation and the History of Religions* (1971); and co-author of *Indian and Far Eastern Religious Traditions* (1972).

He is also author of numerous journal articles, including "Interpretative Categories and the History of Religions" (1968); "Human Rights Priorities and Indian Religious Thought" (1969);

"Factual Statements and the Possibility of Objectivity in History" (1969); "Normative Elements in Eliade's Phenomenology of Symbolism" (1970); "The Symbol of Emptiness and the Emptiness of Symbols" (1972); "Mr. Justice Gajendragadkar and the Religion of the Indian Secular State" (1972); and "Religion and the Secular: Categories for Religious Conflict and Religious Change in Independent India" (1975).

He has done field work in India on two occasions: in 1966 as a Postdoctoral Fellow in Asian Religions (S.R.H.E.), and in 1972 as a Faculty Fellow of the American Institute of Indian Studies.